SIDE *by* SIDE

SECONDARY SCHOOL EDITION

BOOK
2

Steven J. Molinsky • Bill Bliss

PRENTICE HALL REGENTS
A VIACOM COMPANY

Upper Saddle River, New Jersey 07458

Publisher: *Tina Carver*
Director of Production and Manufacturing: *Aliza Greenblatt*
Editorial Production/Design Manager: *Paul Belfanti*
Production Supervision: *Kelly Tavares* and *Ken Liao*
Electronic Art: *Todd Ware*
Realia: *Don Kilcoyne*
Production Coordinator: *Dave Dickey*
Cover Coordinator: *Wanda España*

Interior Design: *Kenny Beck*
Cover: *Martha Sedgwick*

Illustrations: *Richard E. Hill*
Photographs: *Paul Tañedo*

PRENTICE HALL REGENTS
A VIACOM COMPANY

© 1996 by Prentice Hall Regents
Prentice-Hall, Inc.
A Simon & Schuster Company
Upper Saddle River, New Jersey 07458

Printed in the United States of America

10 9 8 7 6 5 4 3 2 1   02 01 00 99 98 97 96

ISBN 0-13-440132-8 (paper)
ISBN 0-13-456195-3 (case)

Prentice-Hall International (UK) Limited, *London*
Prentice-Hall of Australia Pty. Limited, *Sydney*
Prentice-Hall Canada Inc., *Toronto*
Prentice-Hall Hispanoamericana, S.A., *Mexico*
Prentice-Hall of India Private Limited, *New Delhi*
Prentice-Hall of Japan, Inc., *Tokyo*
Simon & Schuster Asia Pte. Ltd., *Singapore*
Editora Prentice-Hall do Brasil, Ltda., *Rio de Janeiro*

CONTENTS

Review: Describing Past, Present, and Future Actions ■
Birthdays and Gifts ■
Telling about Friendships ■
Small Talk in the Hall ■

Like to ■
Review of Tenses:
  Simple Present
  Simple Past
  Future: Going to ■
Time Expressions ■
Indirect Object
  Pronouns ■

Are You Going to Cook Spaghetti This Week?

A. Are you going to cook spaghetti this week?

B. No, I'm not.   I cooked spaghetti LAST week,* and I don't like to cook spaghetti very often.

*You can also say:
    yesterday morning, afternoon, evening
    last night
    last week, weekend, month, year
    last Sunday, Monday, . . . Saturday
    last spring, summer, fall (autumn), winter
    last January, February, . . . December

1. Are you going to study English this weekend?

2. Are you going to watch TV tonight?

3. Are you going to drink coffee this morning?

4. Is Robert going to buy new clothes this year?

5. Are you going to have dessert this evening?

6. Is Tommy going to play baseball this Saturday?

7. Is Mr. Peterson going to plant flowers this spring?

8. Is Mrs. Johnson going to clean her apartment this week?

9. Are you going skiing* this February?

10. Is Linda going to travel to Canada this August?

11. Are Mr. and Mrs. Smith going to London this summer?

12. Are you and your friends going to Miami this winter?

*Going skiing = going to go skiing

3

What Are You Going to Give Your Wife for Her Birthday?

> I'm going to give my wife a present.
> I'm going to give   her   a present.

A. What are you going to give your wife for her birthday?

B. I don't know.   I can't give her a necklace.   I gave her a necklace LAST YEAR.

A. How about flowers?

B. No.   I can't give her flowers.   I gave her flowers TWO YEARS AGO.

A. Well, what are you going to give her?

B. I don't know.   I really have to think about it.

A. What are you going to give your _____ for (his/her) birthday?

B. I don't know.   I can't _____.   I _____ LAST YEAR.

A. How about _____?

B. No.   I can't _____.   I _____TWO YEARS AGO.

A. Well, what are you going to give (him/her)?

B. I don't know.   I really have to think about it.

1. *husband*
   a new shirt
   a necktie

2. *girlfriend*
   perfume
   a bracelet

3. *boyfriend*
   a belt
   a sweater

4. *grandmother*
   flowers
   candy

5. *daughter*
   a bicycle
   a doll

6.

Harry!　I'm Really Upset!

Why Was She Upset with Harry?

1. He didn't _____ flowers.
2. _____ candy.
3. _____ a present.
4. _____ "Happy Birthday."

ON YOUR OWN:　Birthdays

> January 23rd = January twenty-third
> November 16th = November sixteenth
> December 31st = December thirty-first

When is your birthday?
(My birthday is _____.)

Tell about your last birthday:

What did you do?
Did you receive any presents?
What did you get?
Did your family or friends do
　anything special for you?
What did they do?

VERY GOOD FRIENDS: EAST AND WEST

Tom and Janet are very good friends. They grew up together, they went to high school together, and they went to college together. Now Tom lives in San Diego, and Janet lives in Philadelphia. Even though they live far apart, they're still very good friends.

They write to each other very often. He writes her letters about life on the West Coast, and she writes him letters about life on the East Coast. They never forget each other's birthdays. Last year he sent her a silver bracelet, and she sent him a silk necktie. Tom and Janet help each other very often. Last year he lent her money when she was in the hospital, and she gave him advice when he lost his job.

Tom and Janet like each other very much. They were always very good friends, and they still are.

VERY GOOD FRIENDS: NORTH AND SOUTH

Walter and Linda are our very good friends. For many years we went to church together, we took vacations together, and our children played together. Now Walter and Linda live in Alabama, and we still live here in Minnesota. Even though we live far apart, we're still very good friends.

We write to each other very often. We write them letters about life up north, and they write us letters about life down south. We never forget each other's anniversaries. Last year we sent them a plant, and they sent us a painting. We also help each other very often. Last year we lent them money when they bought a new car, and they gave us advice when we sold our house and moved into an apartment.

We like each other very much. We were always good friends, and we still are.

☑ CHECK-UP

True or False?

1. Tom and Janet are in college.
2. Tom lives on the West Coast.
3. Janet was sick last year.
4. Janet sent Tom a silver bracelet last year.
5. They were friends when they were children.
6. Walter and Linda don't live in Minnesota now.
7. Alabama is in the north.
8. Minnesota and Alabama are far apart.
9. Walter and Linda bought a new car last year.
10. Even though Walter and Linda live far apart from their friends, they're still very good friends.

Choose

What word *doesn't* belong?

	a.	b.	c.	d.
1.	grandmother	boyfriend	girlfriend	daughter
2.	sweater	necktie	belt	doll
3.	east	north	coast	south
4.	morning	night	weekend	afternoon
5.	last year	tomorrow morning	three years ago	yesterday

Listening

Listen and choose the best answer.

1. a. I like to cook spaghetti.
   b. I'm going to cook spaghetti.

2. a. I gave him a watch.
   b. I'm going to give him a necktie.

3. a. Yesterday afternoon.
   b. Tomorrow morning.

4. a. I went skiing.
   b. I go skiing.

5. a. They went to Rome.
   b. They're going to Miami.

6. a. They wrote every week.
   b. They write every week.

7. a. He sent her flowers.
   b. He sends her candy.

8. a. Last weekend.
   b. Tomorrow morning.

IN YOUR OWN WORDS

For Writing and Discussion

A VERY GOOD FRIEND

Do you have a very good friend who lives far away? Tell about your friendship.

How do you know each other?
How often do you write to/call each other?
What do you write about/talk about?
Do you send each other presents?
Do you help each other?   How?

SCHOOL CONNECTIONS: Small Talk in the Hall

A. What do you like to do on the weekend?

B. I like to play soccer with my friends. How about you?

A. I like to work in our garden.

A. What are you going to do this weekend?

B. I'm going to do my book report. How about you?

A. I'm going to baby-sit for my neighbors.

Circulate around the classroom. Talk with lots of students. Make a new friend!

A. What do you like to do on the weekend?
B. I like to _____. How about you?
A. I like to _____.

A. What are you going to do this weekend?
B. I'm going to _____. How about you?
A. I'm going to _____.

2

Food ■
Buying Food ■
Describing Food
    Preferences ■
Being a Guest at
    Mealtime ■
Cafeteria Food ■

Count/Non-Count
Nouns ■

What's in Henry's Kitchen?

Count Nouns	Non-Count Nouns
tomatoes	*cheese*
eggs	*milk*
bananas	*ice cream*
apples	*bread*

Add foods from YOUR kitchen.

Let's Make Sandwiches for Lunch!

Let's make sandwiches for lunch!

Sorry, we can't. There **isn't** any **bread**.

Let's make an apple pie for dessert!

Sorry, we can't. There **aren't** any **apples**.

1. **A.** Let's make a salad for dinner!
   B. Sorry, _____. _____ lettuce.

2. **A.** Let's make an omelette for breakfast!
   B. Sorry, _____. _____ eggs.

3. **A.** Let's make some fresh lemonade!
   B. Sorry, _____. _____ lemons.

4. **A.** Let's bake a cake for dessert!
   B. Sorry, _____. _____ flour.

5. **A.** Let's make pizza for lunch!
   B. Sorry, _____. _____ cheese.

6. **A.** Let's make some fresh orange juice for breakfast!
   B. Sorry, _____. _____ oranges.

7. **A.** Let's make chicken and rice for dinner!
   B. Sorry, _____. _____ chicken.

8. **A.** Let's have french fries with our hamburgers!
   B. Sorry, _____. _____ potatoes.

9. **A.** Let's _____!
   B. Sorry, _____. _____.

How Much Milk Do You Want?

how much?	how many?
too much	too many
a little	a few

A. How much milk do you want?

B. Not too much.   Just a little.

A. Okay.   Here you are.

B. Thanks.

A. How many cookies do you want?

B. Not too many.   Just a few.

A. Okay.   Here you are.

B. Thanks.

1. *coffee*

2. *french fries*

3. *ice cream*

4. *rice*

5. *meatballs*

6.

ON YOUR OWN: Would You Care for Some More?

A. How do you like the _____?

B. I think (it's/they're) delicious.

A. I'm glad you like (it/them).   Would you care for some more?

B. Yes, please.   But not (too much/too many).   Just (a little/a few).
My doctor says that (too much/too many)_____ (is/are) bad for my health.

Practice this conversation with other students in your class, using these foods and others.

1. *potatoes*

2. *chocolate cake*

3. *ice cream*

4. *cookies*

5.

TWO BAGS OF GROCERIES

Henry is at the supermarket and he's really upset. He just bought some groceries, and he can't believe he just spent forty dollars! He bought only a few oranges, a few apples, a little milk, a little ice cream, and a few eggs.

He also bought just a little coffee, a few onions, a few bananas, a little rice, a little cheese, and a few lemons. He didn't buy very much fish, he didn't buy very many grapes, and he didn't buy very much meat.

Henry just spent forty dollars, but he's walking out of the supermarket with only two bags of groceries. No wonder he's upset!

✓ CHECK-UP

Q & A

Using these models, make questions and answers based on the story.

A. How many *oranges* did he buy?
B. He bought only a few *oranges*.

A. How much *milk* did he buy?
B. He bought only a little *milk*.

How about YOU?

What did YOU buy the last time you went to the supermarket?

(I bought a few . . . /a little . . .)

Listening

Listen and choose what the people are talking about.

1.	a. ice cream	b. cookies		5.	a. eggs	b. butter
2.	a. chicken	b. potatoes		6.	a. salad	b. french fries
3.	a. meatballs	b. orange juice		7.	a. apples	b. rice
4.	a. cake	b. bananas		8.	a. lemonade	b. lemons

14

DELICIOUS!

Peter likes chocolate chip cookies. In fact, he eats them all the time. His friends often tell him that he eats too many chocolate chip cookies, but Peter doesn't think so. He thinks they're delicious.

Gloria likes coffee. In fact, she drinks it all the time. Her doctor often tells her that she drinks too much coffee, but Gloria doesn't think so. She thinks it's delicious.

TASTES TERRIBLE!

Sally doesn't like vegetables. In fact, she never eats them. Her parents often tell her that vegetables are good for her, but Sally doesn't care. She thinks they taste terrible.

Michael doesn't like yogurt. In fact, he never eats it. His daughter often tells him that yogurt is good for him, but Michael doesn't care. He thinks it tastes terrible.

IN YOUR OWN WORDS

For Writing and Discussion

Tell about foods you like.

What foods do you think are delicious?
How often do you eat them?
Are they good for you or are they bad for you?
Do you think you eat too many or too much of them?

Tell about foods you don't like.

What foods do you think taste terrible?
How often do you eat them?
Are they good for you or are they bad for you?

SCHOOL CONNECTIONS: Cafeteria Food

A. How are the french fries?

B. They're okay. How's the fajita?

A. It's pretty good.

A. How's the sandwich?

B. It's delicious! How are the baked beans?

A. They're awful!

Make a list of food items in your school cafeteria.

Count Noun Cafeteria Food		Non-Count Noun Cafeteria Food	
_____	_____	_____	_____
_____	_____	_____	_____
_____	_____	_____	_____

Now circulate around the classroom. Practice lunchroom conversations about food with other students. Then practice in the cafeteria!

A. How (is / are) the _____?

B. (It's / They're) _____. How (is / are) the _____?

A. (It's / They're) _____.

Buying Food ■
Describing Food ■
Eating in a Restaurant ■
Recipes ■
Computers: The Keyboard ■

Partitives ■
Count/Non-Count
Nouns ■
Imperatives ■

Do We Need Anything from the Supermarket?

My Shopping List

a can of beans
a jar of jam
a bottle of soda
a box of cereal
a bag of flour
a loaf of white bread
2 loaves of whole wheat bread
a bunch of bananas
2 bunches of carrots
a head of lettuce

a lb.* of butter
½ lb.* of cheese

a quart of milk
a dozen eggs

*A lb. = a pound; ½ lb. = a half pound, or half a pound.

A. Do we need anything from the supermarket?

B. Yes.   We need a loaf of bread.

A. A loaf of bread?

B. Yes.

A. Anything else?

B. No.   Just a loaf of bread.

1. *cereal*

2. *jam*

3. *soda*

4. *bananas*

5. *vegetable soup*

6. *whole wheat bread*

7. *flour*

8.

How about YOU?

What did YOU buy the last time you went shopping?

How Much Does a Head of Lettuce Cost?

A. How much does **a head of lettuce** cost?

B. **Ninety-five cents** (95¢).*

A. NINETY-FIVE CENTS?!   That's a lot of money!

B. You're right.   **Lettuce** is very expensive this week.

*25¢ = twenty-five cents
 50¢ = fifty cents
     etc.

A. How much does **a pound of apples** cost?

B. **A dollar twenty-five** ($1.25).†

A. A DOLLAR TWENTY-FIVE?!   That's a lot of money!

B. You're right.   **Apples** are very expensive this week.

†$1.00 = a dollar $2.25 = two twenty-five
 $1.50 = a dollar fifty $4.50 = four fifty
              etc.

1. *butter*

2. *carrots*

3. *milk*

4. *onions*

5. *Swiss cheese*

6. *soda*

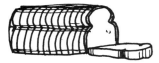

7. *white bread*

8. *oranges*

9.

READING

NOTHING TO EAT FOR DINNER

Joan had to work overtime at the office today. She got home late, and she was hungry. When she opened the refrigerator, she was very upset. There was nothing to eat for dinner. Joan sat down and wrote a shopping list. She needed a head of lettuce, a bunch of bananas, a quart of milk, a dozen eggs, two pounds of tomatoes, a pound of butter, two bunches of carrots, and a loaf of bread.

Joan rushed out of the house and drove to the supermarket. When she got there, she was very disappointed. There wasn't any lettuce. There weren't any bananas. There wasn't any milk. There weren't any eggs. There weren't any tomatoes. There wasn't any butter. There weren't any carrots, and there wasn't any bread.

Joan was tired and upset. In fact, she was so tired and upset that she lost her appetite, drove home, didn't have dinner, and went to bed.

CHECK-UP

Q & A

Joan is at the supermarket. Using these models, create dialogs based on the story.

A. Excuse me. I'm looking for a *head of lettuce*.
B. Sorry. There isn't any more *lettuce*.
A. There isn't?
B. No, there isn't. Sorry.

A. Excuse me. I'm looking for a *bunch of bananas*.
B. Sorry. There aren't any more *bananas*.
A. There aren't?
B. No, there aren't. Sorry.

Listening

Listen and choose what the people are talking about.

1. a. milk   b. cheese
2. a. bread   b. flour
3. a. carrots   b. lettuce
4. a. onions   b. butter

5. a. eggs   b. milk
6. a. beans   b. rice
7. a. cake   b. oranges
8. a. cereal   b. soda

What Would You Like?

A. What would you like **for dessert?**

B. I can't decide.   What do you recommend?

A. I recommend our **chocolate ice cream.**
Everybody says **it's** delicious.*

B. Okay.   Please give me **a dish of chocolate ice cream.**

A. What would you like **for breakfast?**

B. I can't decide.   What do you recommend?

A. I recommend our **scrambled eggs.**
Everybody says **they're** out of this world.*

B. Okay.   Please give me **an order of scrambled eggs.**

*You can also say: fantastic, wonderful, magnificent, excellent.

What would you like . . .

1. . . . for dessert?
(a piece of) apple pie

2. . . . for lunch?
(a bowl of) chicken soup

3. . . . to drink?
(a cup of) coffee

4. . . . for breakfast?
(an order of) pancakes

5. . . . to drink?
(a glass of) red wine

6. . . . for dessert?
*(a dish of) vanilla
ice cream*

7. . . . to drink?
(a cup of) hot chocolate

8. . . . for dessert?
(a bowl of) strawberries

9.

Stanley's Favorite Recipes

Are you going to have a party soon?   Do you want to cook something special?   Stanley the chef recommends this recipe for VEGETABLE STEW.   This is Stanley's favorite recipe for vegetable stew, and everybody says it's fantastic!

1. Put **a little butter** into a saucepan.

2. Chop up **a few onions**.

3. Cut up (**a little/a few**) _____.

4. Pour in _____.

5. Slice _____.

6. Add _____.

7. Chop up _____.

8. Slice _____.

9. Add _____.

10. Cook for 3 hours.

When is your English teacher's birthday?   Do you want to bake a special cake?   Stanley the chef recommends this recipe for FRUITCAKE.   This is Stanley's favorite recipe for fruitcake, and everybody says it's out of this world!

1. Put 3 cups of flour into a mixing bowl.

2. Add **a little sugar**.

3. Slice (**a little/a few**) _____.

4. Cut up _____.

5. Pour in _____.

6. Add _____.

7. Chop up _____.

8. Add _____.

9. Mix in _____.

10. Bake for 45 minutes.

How about YOU?

Do you have a favorite recipe?
Share it with other students in your class.

READING

AT THE CONTINENTAL RESTAURANT

Yesterday was Sherman and Dorothy Johnson's twenty-third wedding anniversary. They went to the Continental Restaurant for dinner. This restaurant is a very special place for Sherman and Dorothy because they went there on their first date twenty-four years ago.

Sherman and Dorothy sat at a quiet, romantic table in the corner. They had two glasses of wine, and then they ordered dinner. First, Dorothy ordered a bowl of vegetable soup, and Sherman ordered a glass of tomato juice. For the main course, Dorothy ordered baked chicken with rice, and Sherman ordered broiled fish with potatoes. For dessert, Dorothy ordered a piece of apple pie, and Sherman ordered a bowl of strawberries.

Sherman and Dorothy enjoyed their dinner very much. The soup was delicious, and the tomato juice was fresh. The chicken was wonderful, and the rice was tasty. The fish was fantastic, and the potatoes were excellent. The apple pie was magnificent, and the strawberries were out of this world.

Sherman and Dorothy had a wonderful evening at the Continental Restaurant. It was a very special anniversary.

✔ CHECK-UP

Q & A

1. Sherman and Dorothy are at the Continental Restaurant. They're ordering dinner from their waiter or waitress. Using these lines to begin, create a dialog based on the story.

   A. Would you like to order now?
   B. Yes. I'd like ...

2. The waiter or waitress is asking about the dinner. Using this model, create dialogs based on the story.

   A. How *is the vegetable soup?*
   B. *It's delicious*!
   A. I'm glad you like *it*.

How about YOU?

Tell about the last time you went to a restaurant:

Where did you go?   What did you order?
How was the food?   How much did you spend?

COMPUTER CONNECTIONS: The Keyboard

① The **Function keys (F keys)** give commands in many PC programs.

② The **Power On key** on some computers turns on the system.

③ The **typewriter keys** work like the keys on a typewriter.

④ The **Caps Lock key** makes capital (upper case) letters.

⑤ The **Shift key** makes capital letters and the upper characters on other keys (# $ % " ?).

⑥ The **Control key**, the **Option key**, and the **Command key** work in combination with other keys. With these keys you can give special commands and show special characters.

⑦ The **Delete key** deletes (erases) characters to the left of the cursor.

⑧ The **Return key** moves the cursor to the beginning of the next line.

⑨ The **Arrow keys** move the cursor up, down, right, or left—one character at a time.

⑩ The **Numeric keypad** has keys for the digits 0 through 9, addition (+), subtraction (-), multiplication (*), division (/), a decimal point (.), and an equals sign (=).

Keyboards in Your School

What kinds of computers do you have in your school? Are there both PC computers and Macintosh computers?

Compare the keyboards on different computers. How are these keyboards different?

The **cursor** is a little blinking line. It shows your location on the screen. It is also called the **insertion point**.

4

Will the Train Arrive Soon?

(I will)	I'll
(He will)	He'll
(She will)	She'll
(It will)	It'll } work.
(We will)	We'll
(You will)	You'll
(They will)	They'll

Will he work?
Yes, he will.

A. Will the train arrive soon?

B. Yes, it will.   It'll arrive in five minutes.

1. Will the soup be ready soon?
   Yes, _____. _____ in a few minutes.

2. Will Miss Blake return soon?
   Yes, _____. _____ in an hour.

3. Will Dr. Smith be here soon?
   Yes, _____. _____ in half an hour.

4. Will you be ready soon?
   Yes, _____. _____ in a few seconds.

5. Will the tomatoes be ripe soon?
   Yes, _____. _____ in a few weeks.

6. Will the concert begin soon?
   Yes, _____. _____ at seven o'clock.

7. Will Mrs. Green be home soon?
   Yes, _____. _____ in a little while.

8. Will you be back soon?
   Yes, _____. _____ in a week.

9. Will Betty get out of the hospital soon?
   Yes, _____. _____ in a few days.

10. Will Frank get out of jail soon?
    Yes, _____. _____ in a few months.

What Do You Think?

| I He She It We You They | will work. |

| I He She It We You They | won't work. (will not) |

Do you think it'll rain tomorrow?

Maybe it will, and maybe it won't. We'll just have to wait and see.

1. Do you think Cynthia will marry Norman?

2. Do you think it'll be very cold this winter?

3. Do you think you'll be happy in your new neighborhood?

4. Do you think Mary's husband will find a new job?

5. Do you think I'll be famous some day?

6. Do you think they'll have a baby soon?

7. Do you think there will be many people at the beach tomorrow?

8. Do you think we'll have to fight in a war some day?

9. Do you think _____?

I CAN'T WAIT FOR SPRING TO COME!

I'm tired of winter. I'm tired of the snow, I'm tired of cold weather, and I'm sick and tired of winter coats and boots! Just think . . . in a few more weeks it won't be winter any more. It'll be spring. The weather won't be cold. It'll be warm. It won't snow any more. It'll be sunny. I won't have to stay indoors any more. I'll go outside and play with my friends. We'll ride bicycles and play baseball again.

In a few more weeks our neighborhood won't look sad and gray any more. The flowers will bloom, and the trees will become green again. My family will spend more time outdoors. My father will work in the yard. He'll cut the grass and paint the fence. My mother will work in the yard, too. She'll buy new flowers and plant them in the garden. On weekends we won't just sit in the living room and watch TV. We'll go for walks in the park, and we'll have picnics on Sunday afternoons.

I can't wait for spring to come! Hurry, spring!

✓ CHECK-UP

True, False, or Maybe?

Answer True, False, or Maybe (if the answer isn't in the story).

1. It's spring.
2. The boy in the story likes to stay inside during the spring.
3. The boy has a cold.
4. The trees aren't green now.
5. The park is near their house.
6. The boy plays baseball with his friends all year.
7. The family has a TV in their living room.
8. The boy's family doesn't like the winter.

How about YOU?

What's your favorite season? Spring? Summer? Fall? Winter? What's the weather like in your favorite season? What do you like to do?

They Really Can't Decide

I
He
She
It
We
You
They
} might clean it today.

A. When are you going to clean your apartment?

B. I don't know. I might clean it today, or I might clean it next Saturday. I really can't decide.

A. Where are you going to go for your vacation?

B. We don't know. We might go to Mexico, or we might go to Japan. We really can't decide.

1. What is he going to cook tonight?

2. What color is she going to paint her kitchen?

3. What are they going to name their new daughter?

4. When are you two going to get married?

5. What are you going to buy your brother for his birthday?

6. What are they going to do tonight?

7. How are you going to come to class tomorrow?

8. What's he going to name his new puppy?

9. What are you going to be when you grow up?

Careful!

A. Careful! Put on your helmet!

B. I'm sorry. What did you say?

A. Put on your helmet! You might hurt your head.

B. Oh. Thanks for the warning.

1. The floor is wet!
   fall

2. Don't stand there!
   get hit

3. Don't smoke in here!
   start a fire

4. Put on your safety glasses!
   hurt your eyes

5. Don't touch the machine!
   get hurt

6.

I'm Afraid I Might Drown

A. Would you like to go swimming with me?*

B. No, I don't think so.

A. Why not?

B. I'm afraid I might drown.

A. Don't worry!   You won't drown.

B. Are you sure?

A. I'm positive!

B. Okay.   I'll go swimming with you.

*Or: Do you want to go swimming with me?

1. *go skiing*
    break my leg

2. *go to a fancy restaurant*
    get sick

3. *go to the beach*
    get a sunburn

4. *go dancing*
    step on your feet

5. *take a walk in the park*
    catch a cold

6. *go to Jack's party*
    have a terrible time

7. *go sailing*
    get seasick

8. *take a ride in the*
       country
    get carsick

9. *go to the movies*
    fall asleep

10. _____

JUST IN CASE

Larry didn't go to work today, and he might not go to work tomorrow either. He might see his doctor instead. He's feeling absolutely terrible, and he thinks he might have pneumonia. Larry isn't positive, but he doesn't want to take any chances. He thinks it might be a good idea for him to see his doctor . . . just in case.

Mrs. Randall didn't go to the office today, and she might not go to the office tomorrow either. She might go to the doctor instead. She feels nauseous every morning, and she thinks she might be pregnant. Mrs. Randall isn't positive, but she doesn't want to take any chances. She thinks it might be a good idea for her to go to the doctor . . . just in case.

Tommy and Julie Harris didn't go to school today, and they might not go to school tomorrow either. They might stay home in bed instead. They have little red spots all over their arms and legs. Mr. and Mrs. Harris think their children might have the measles. They aren't positive, but they don't want to take any chances. They think it might be a good idea for Tommy and Julie to stay home in bed . . . just in case.

✓ CHECK-UP

Choose

Larry is "calling in sick." Choose the correct words and then practice the conversation.

A. Hello. This is Larry. I $\boxed{\begin{array}{c}\text{might}\\\text{can't}\end{array}}^1$ come to work today. I think I $\boxed{\begin{array}{c}\text{will}\\\text{might}\end{array}}^2$ have pneumonia.

B. That's too bad. $\boxed{\begin{array}{c}\text{Are you}\\\text{Will you}\end{array}}^3$ going to see your doctor?

A. I'm not sure. I think I $\boxed{\begin{array}{c}\text{might}\\\text{will}\end{array}}^4$.

B. $\boxed{\begin{array}{c}\text{Not}\\\text{Will}\end{array}}^5$ you be at work tomorrow?

A. I'm not sure. I $\boxed{\begin{array}{c}\text{might not}\\\text{might}\end{array}}^6$ go to work tomorrow either.

B. Well, I hope you feel better soon.

A. Thanks.

Listening

I. Mrs. Harris is calling Tommy and Julie's school. Listen and choose the correct lines for Mrs. Harris.

1. a. Hello. This is Mrs. Harris.
   b. Hello. This is the Park Elementary School.
2. a. I can't.
   b. Tommy and Julie won't be in school today.
3. a. They might have the measles.
   b. Yes. This is their mother.
4. a. They aren't bad. They're just sick.
   b. Yes.
5. a. Thank you.
   b. It might be a good idea.

II. Choose the word you hear.

1. a. will   b. we'll
2. a. won't   b. want to
3. a. here   b. there
4. a. they   b. they'll

5. a. hurt   b. hit
6. a. I'll   b. I
7. a. wet   b. red
8. a. sick   b. seasick

IN YOUR OWN WORDS

For Writing and Discussion

You didn't go to work or school today, and you might not go tomorrow either. Write a note to your boss or teacher and explain why. (A friend will deliver the note for you.)

_____, 19 ___

Dear _____,

    I'm sorry I didn't come to _____ today. I'm feeling ....
....
....

    I'll return to _____ very soon. I hope you understand.

             Sincerely,

             _____

COMPUTER CONNECTIONS: The Mouse and the Trackball

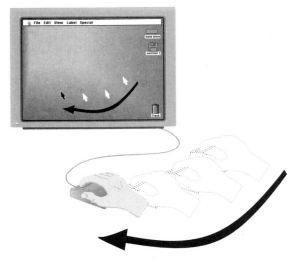

The mouse is an important part of the computer. It moves a pointer on the computer screen.

If you move the mouse forward, the pointer will move up the screen.

If you move the mouse backward, the pointer will move down the screen.

If you move the mouse to the right or left, the pointer will move to the right or left.

There is a ball at the bottom of the mouse. If the ball doesn't move, the pointer won't move. If you lift the mouse, you won't move the pointer. So if you don't have room to move the mouse, lift the mouse and put it down in a different place.

A trackball works like a mouse, but the ball is on top. You roll the ball to move the pointer on the screen.

MOUSE COMMANDS

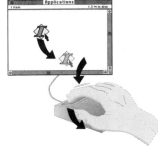

click
Press and release the button.

double-click
Press and release the button twice.

press
Press and hold down the button.

drag
Press and hold down the button, and move the mouse.

COMPUTER LAB

Practice with the mouse or trackball on a computer in your school.

Move the mouse on the table forward, backward, right, and left. What happens to the pointer on the screen?

Lift the mouse. What happens on the screen?

Practice the mouse commands.

Making Comparisons ■

Advice ■

Parents and Children ■

Comparing Life in Different
  Places ■

Expressing Opinions ■

Expressing Agreement
  and Disagreement ■

Computers: Ergonomics ■

Comparatives ■

Should ■

Possessive Pronouns ■

My New Apartment Is Larger

| cold – colder | large – larger | big – bigger | easy – easier |
| short – shorter | safe – safer | hot – hotter | busy – busier |

A. I think you'll like my new apartment.

B. But I liked your OLD apartment.   It was **large.**

A. That's right.   But my new apartment is **larger.**

1. *bicycle*
   fast

2. *refrigerator*
   big

3. *dog*
   friendly

4. *neighborhood*
   safe

5. *living room rug*
   soft

6. *sports car*
   fancy

7. *tennis racket*
   light

8. *recipe for vegetable stew*
   easy

9. *wig*
   pretty

My New Rocking Chair Is More Comfortable

cold – colder	interesting – more interesting
large – larger	intelligent – more intelligent
big – bigger	comfortable – more comfortable
easy – easier	beautiful – more beautiful

A. I think you'll like my new rocking chair.

B. But I liked your OLD rocking chair.   It was **comfortable**.

A. That's right.   But my new rocking chair is **more comfortable**.

1. *girlfriend*
   intelligent

2. *boyfriend*
   handsome

3. *house*
   beautiful

4. *kitchen sink*
   large

5. *sofa*
   attractive

6. *English teacher*
   smart

7. *roommate*
   interesting

8. *boss*
   nice

9. *computer*
   powerful

10. *air conditioner*
    quiet

11. *recipe for fruitcake*
    delicious

12. I pod
    nice

BROWNSVILLE

The Taylor family lived in Brownsville for many years. And for many years, Brownsville was a very good place to live. The streets were clean. The parks were safe. The bus system was reliable, and the schools were good.

But Brownsville changed. Today the streets aren't as clean as they used to be. The parks aren't as safe as they used to be. The bus system isn't as reliable as it used to be, and the schools aren't as good as they used to be.

Because of the changes in Brownsville, the Taylor family moved to Newport last year. In Newport the streets are cleaner. The parks are safer. The bus system is more reliable, and the schools are better. The Taylors are happy in Newport, but they were happier in Brownsville. Although Newport has cleaner streets, safer parks, a more reliable bus system, and better schools, Brownsville has friendlier people. They're nicer, more polite, and more hospitable than the people in Newport.

The Taylors miss Brownsville. Even though they're now living in Newport, Brownsville will always be their real home.

✔ CHECK-UP

Q & A

The people of Brownsville are calling Mayor Brown's radio talk show. They're upset about Brownsville's streets, parks, bus system, and schools. Using this model and the story, call Mayor Brown.

A. This is Mayor Brown. You're on the air.

B. Mayor Brown, I'm very upset about the *streets* here in Brownsville.

A. Why?

B. *They aren't* as *clean* as *they* used to be.

A. Do you really think so?

B. Definitely! You know . . . they say the *streets* in Newport *are cleaner.*

A. I'll see what I can do. Thank you for calling.

Bicycles Are Safer Than Motorcycles

I
He
She
It } should study.   Should I study?
We
You
They

A. Should I buy a bicycle or a motorcycle?

B. I think you should buy a bicycle.

A. Why?*

B. Bicycles are **safer than** motorcycles.

A. Should he study English or Latin?

B. I think he should study English.

A. Why?*

B. English is **more useful than** Latin.

*Or: Why do you say that?   What makes you say that?   How come?

1. Should I buy a dog or a cat?

2. Should he buy a used car or a new car?

3. Should I vote for John Black or Peter Smith?

4. Should he go out on a date with Doris or Jane?

5. Should she go out on a date with Roger or Bill?

6. Should they buy a black-and-white TV or a color TV?

7. Should we buy this fan or that fan?

9. Should I plant flowers or vegetables this spring?

11. Should I buy the hat in my left hand or the hat in my right hand?

13. Should she buy fur gloves or leather gloves?

15. Should I hire Miss Jones or Miss Wilson?

8. Should she buy these earrings or those earrings?

10. Should he study the piano with Mrs. Wong or Miss Schultz?

12. Should they go to the cafeteria up the street or the cafeteria down the street?

14. Should I go to the laundromat across the street or the laundromat around the corner?

16. Should I fire Mr. Jackson or Mr. Brown?

17.

READING

IT ISN'T EASY BEING A TEENAGER

I try to be a good son, but no matter how hard I try, my parents never seem to be satisfied. They think I should eat healthier food, I should wear nicer clothes, and I should get better grades. And according to them, my hair should be shorter, my room should be neater, and my friends should be more polite when they come to visit.

You know . . . it isn't easy being a teenager.

IT ISN'T EASY BEING PARENTS

We try to be good parents, but no matter how hard we try, our children never seem to be satisfied. They think we should wear more fashionable clothes, we should buy a faster car, and we should listen to more interesting music. And according to them, we should be more sympathetic when they talk about their problems, we should be friendlier when their friends come to visit, and we should be more understanding when they come home late from a Saturday night date.

You know . . . it isn't easy being parents.

 *CHECK-UP*

Choose

What word *doesn't* belong?

1.	a.	sympathetic	b.	fancy	c.	understanding	d.	friendly
2.	a.	clean	b.	convenient	c.	soft	d.	safe
3.	a.	honest	b.	intelligent	c.	reliable	d.	lazy
4.	a.	large	b.	capable	c.	intelligent	d.	talented
5.	a.	friendly	b.	useful	c.	hospitable	d.	polite

Listening

Listen and choose what the people are talking about.

1.	a.	hair	b.	room	4.	a.	car	b.	earring
2.	a.	tennis racket	b.	car	5.	a.	grades	b.	schools
3.	a.	friends	b.	clothes	6.	a.	TV	b.	motorcycle

Don't Be Ridiculous!

my – mine	our – ours
his – his	your – yours
her – hers	their – theirs

A. You know, my dog isn't as friendly as your dog.

B. Don't be ridiculous! Yours is MUCH friendlier than **mine.**

A. You know, my novels aren't as interesting as Ernest Hemingway's novels.

B. Don't be ridiculous! Yours are MUCH more interesting than **his.**

fast

1. *my car*
   your car

comfortable

2. *my furniture*
   your furniture

nice

3. *my boss*
   your boss

intelligent

4. *my children*
   your children

big

5. *my house*
   the Jones's house

clean

6. *my apartment*
   your apartment

good-better

7. *my pronunciation*
   Maria's pronunciation

important

8. *my job*
   the President's job

9.

ON YOUR OWN: Cities

In my opinion, New York is more interesting than San Francisco.

I disagree. I think San Francisco is MUCH more interesting than New York.

Do you think the weather in Miami is better than the weather in Honolulu?

No, I don't think so. I think the weather in Honolulu is MUCH better than the weather in Miami.

Are the people in Centerville as friendly as the people in Greenville?

No, but they're more interesting. Don't you agree?

Yes, I agree.

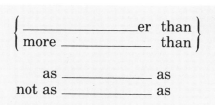

{ _____er than }
{ more _____ than }

as _____ as
not as _____ as

Talk with other students about two cities: your home town and the city you live in now, or any two cities you know. Talk about . . .

the streets: quiet, safe, clean, wide, busy . . . ?
the buildings: high, modern, pretty . . . ?
the weather: cold, warm, rainy, snowy . . . ?
the people: friendly, nice, polite, honest, busy, happy, hospitable,
           talkative, healthy, wealthy, poor . . . ?
the city in general: large, interesting, lively, exciting, expensive . . . ?

In your conversation you might want to use some of these expressions:

Do you think . . . ?
Don't you agree?

I agree.
I disagree.
I agree/disagree with (you, him,
    her, John . . .).

I think so.
I don't think so.
In my opinion, . . .

COMPUTER CONNECTIONS: Ergonomics

You should be comfortable at the computer. Follow these rules of **ergonomics**—the science of how people and things work together.

The top of the monitor should be at eye level or just below eye level.

Your wrists should be straight. They should be at the same level as your elbows, or they should be just a little lower than your elbows.

The back of the keyboard should be higher than the front of the keyboard. Some keyboards are made like this. Other keyboards have tabs on the bottom. Pull out the tabs and the back of the keyboard will be higher.

Lights in the room should not reflect on the screen. This causes **glare**. Don't sit at the computer for too long. Rest your eyes. Get up and move around!

Read each problem of ergonomics. Then choose the correct word to find the solution.

Problem	Solution
1. The top of the monitor is much higher than your eye level.	Your chair should be ((higher) lower).
2. The top of the monitor is much lower than your eye level.	Your chair should be (higher lower).
3. Your elbows are much higher than your wrists.	Your chair should be (higher lower).
4. Your elbows are much lower than your wrists.	Your chair should be (higher lower).
5. There is glare on the screen.	The lights near the computer should be (brighter lower).

Computers In Your School

Where are the computers in your school?
Are the chairs at the computers comfortable? Can you adjust them up and down?

Describing Character Traits ■   Superlatives ■
Shopping in a Department
    Store ■
Describing Products ■
Telling about Your Country:
    People, Places, and Popular
    Culture ■
Discussing Opinions ■
Surveys and Bar Graphs ■

The Smartest Person I Know

kind – the kindest	nice – the nicest
cold – the coldest	safe – the safest
busy – the busiest	big – the biggest
happy – the happiest	hot – the hottest

A. I think your friend Margaret is very **smart**.

B. She certainly is. She's **the smartest** person I know.

1. *your cousin*
   friendly

2. *your Uncle George*
   funny

3. *your parents*
   kind

4. *your older brother*
   shy

5. *your cousin Nancy*
   pretty

6. *Larry*
   lazy

7. *the students in our class*
   nice

8. *your Aunt Gertrude*
   cold

9. *your younger brother*
   sloppy

The Most Energetic Person I Know

kind – the kindest	talented – the most talented
busy – the busiest	energetic – the most energetic
nice – the nicest	interesting – the most interesting
big – the biggest	polite – the most polite

A. I think your grandmother is very **energetic.**

B. She certainly is.   She's **the most energetic** person I know.

1. *your son*
   polite

2. *John*
   stubborn

3. *our English teacher*
   patient

4. *your older sister*
   bright

5. *your younger sister*
   talented

6. *your upstairs neighbor*
   noisy

7. *your downstairs neighbor*
   boring

8. *your twin brothers*
   nice

9. *your grandfather*
   generous

10. *Walter*
    stingy

11. *your girlfriend*
    honest

12.

THE NICEST PERSON

Mr. and Mrs. Jackson are very proud of their daughter, Linda. She's a very nice person. She's friendly, she's polite, she's smart, and she's talented. She's also very pretty.

Mr. and Mrs. Jackson's friends and neighbors always compliment them about Linda. They say she's the nicest person they know. According to them, she's the friendliest, the most polite, the smartest, and the most talented girl in the neighborhood. They also think she's the prettiest.

Mr. and Mrs. Jackson agree. They think Linda is a wonderful girl, and they're proud to say she's their daughter.

THE MOST OBNOXIOUS DOG

Mr. and Mrs. Hubbard are very embarrassed by their dog, Rex. He's a very obnoxious dog. He's noisy, he's stubborn, he's lazy, and he's mean. He's also very ugly.

Mr. and Mrs. Hubbard's friends and neighbors always complain about Rex. They say he's the most obnoxious dog they know. According to them, he's the noisiest, the most stubborn, the laziest, and the meanest dog in the neighborhood. They also think he's the ugliest.

Mr. and Mrs. Hubbard agree. They think Rex is a miserable dog, and they're ashamed to say he's theirs.

CHECK-UP

Q & A

The neighbors are talking. Using these models, create dialogs based on the stories.

A. You know . . . I think Linda is very *nice.*

B. I agree. She the *nicest* girl in the neighborhood.

A. You know . . . I think Rex is very *obnoxious.*

B. You're right. He's the *most obnoxious* dog in the neighborhood.

Tell about the nicest person you know.

I Want to Buy a Small Radio

a small radio	a comfortable chair	a good car
a smaller radio	a more comfortable chair	a better car
the smallest radio	the most comfortable chair	the best car

A. May I help you?

B. Yes, please.   I want to buy a **small** radio.

A. I think you'll like this one.   It's VERY **small.**

B. Don't you have a **smaller** one?

A. No, I'm afraid not.   This is **the smallest** one we have.

B. Thank you anyway.

A. Sorry we can't help you.   Please come again.

A. May I help you?

B. Yes, please.   I want to buy a/an _____ _____.

A. I think you'll like this one.   It's VERY _____.

B. Don't you have a/an { _____er } one?
   { more _____ }

A. No, I'm afraid not.   This is the { _____est } one we have.
   { most _____ }

B. Thank you anyway.

A. Sorry we can't help you.   Please come again.

1. *large refrigerator*

2. *comfortable rocking chair*

3. *good record player*

4. *fancy necktie*

5. *cheap watch*

6. *small kitchen table*

7. *good tape recorder*

8. *light tennis racket*

9. *elegant evening gown*

10. *modern sofa*

11. *short novel*

12.

BOB'S BARGAIN DEPARTMENT STORE

Bob's Bargain Department Store is the cheapest store in town. However, even though it's the cheapest, it isn't the most popular. People don't shop there very often because the products are bad. In fact, some people say the products there are the worst in town.

The furniture isn't very comfortable, the clothes aren't very fashionable, the appliances aren't very dependable, and the record players and tape recorders aren't very good. Besides that, the location isn't very convenient, and the salespeople aren't very helpful.

That's why people don't often shop at Bob's Bargain Department Store, even though it's the cheapest store in town.

THE LORD AND LADY DEPARTMENT STORE

The Lord and Lady Department Store sells very good products. In fact, some people say the products there are the best in town.

They sell the most comfortable furniture, the most fashionable clothes, the most dependable appliances, and the best record players and tape recorders. And besides that, their location is the most convenient, and their salespeople are the most helpful in town.

However, even though the Lord and Lady Department Store is the best store in town, people don't often shop there because it's also the most expensive.

THE SUPER SAVER DEPARTMENT STORE

The Super Saver Department Store is the most popular store in town. It isn't the cheapest, and it isn't the most expensive. It doesn't have the best products, and it doesn't have the worst.

The furniture isn't the most comfortable you can buy, but it's more comfortable than the furniture at many other stores. The clothes aren't the most fashionable you can buy, but they're more fashionable than the clothes at many other stores. The appliances aren't the most dependable you can buy, but they're more dependable than the appliances at many other stores. The record players and tape recorders aren't the best you can buy, but they're better than the record players and tape recorders at many other stores. In addition, the location is convenient, and the salespeople are helpful.

You can see why the Super Saver Department Store is the most popular store in town. The prices are reasonable, and the products are good. That's why people like to shop there.

 *CHECK-UP* _____

True or False?

1. Bob's Bargain Department Store is the most popular store in town.
2. The salespeople at Lord and Lady are more helpful than the salespeople at Super Saver.
3. The location of Lord and Lady isn't as convenient as the location of Bob's.
4. Super Saver has the best prices in town.
5. People in this town say the cheapest department store is the best.

Listening: *A Radio Commercial*

Listen and choose the best answers to complete the commercial.

1. a. cheap   b. expensive
2. a. fashionable   b. convenient
3. a. comfortable   b. dependable
4. a. helpful   b. stubborn
5. a. better   b. best

How about YOU?

Tell about places to shop where you live: the cheapest, the most expensive, the most popular. Tell about the products they sell.

ON YOUR OWN: In Your Opinion

good	bad
better	worse
best	worst

Ask and answer these questions with another student in your class. Give reasons for your opinions.

In your opinion . . .

1. Who is the most popular actor/actress in your country?

2. Who is the most popular TV star?

3. Who is the best singer? (What kind of songs does he/she sing?)

4. Who is the most important person in your country now? (What does he/she do?)

5. Who is the most important person in the history of your country? (What did he/she do?)

In your opinion . . .

6. What is the best city in your country? Why?

7. What is the worst city in your country? Why?

8. What are the most interesting tourist sights for visitors to your country? (museums, monuments, churches . . .)

9. What are the most popular vacation places for people in your country? Why?

In your opinion . . .

10. What is the most popular car in your country?

11. What is the most popular sport?

12. What is the funniest TV program?

13. What is the best newspaper?

14. What is the most popular magazine?

15. What is the most popular food?

SCHOOL CONNECTIONS: Surveys and Bar Graphs

THE MOST POPULAR TV PROGRAMS

These students are taking a survey. They're finding out the favorite TV programs of students in their class. They tally the number of students. Then they draw the information on a bar graph.

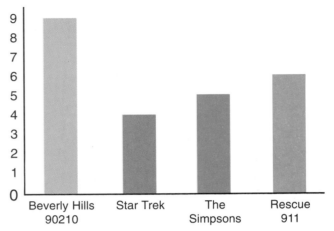

Work with a partner. Take a survey in class about one of these popular forms of entertainment. Circulate around the room. Ask all the students for their opinions. Tally the results. Show the information on the bar graph. Then present your information to the class.

TV program	video game	book
kind of music	computer software	movie
music group	magazine	video

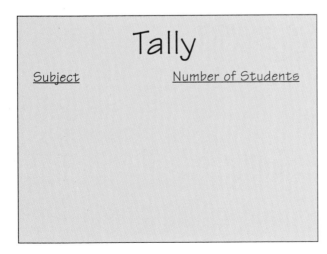

Getting Around Town ■
Public Transportation ■
Following Written Directions to
    a Place ■
Drawing a Map and Writing
    Directions ■
Making Recommendations ■
Computers: The Macintosh
    Desktop ■

Directions ■

Can You Tell Me How to Get to the Laundromat from Here?

walk up walk down walk along	on the right on the left	next to across from between

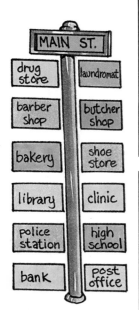

A. Excuse me.   Can you tell me how to get to the laundromat from here?

B. Sure.   **Walk up** Main Street and you'll see the laundromat **on the right, across from** the drug store.

A. Thank you.

laundromat?

A. Excuse me.   Can you tell me how to get to the post office from here?

B. Sure.   **Walk down** Main Street and you'll see the post office **on the left, next to** the high school.

A. Thank you.

post office?

1. *shoe store?*

2. *police station?*

3. *high school?*

4. *barber shop?*

5. *butcher shop?*

6. *bank?*

Could You Please Tell Me How to Get to the Hospital from Here?

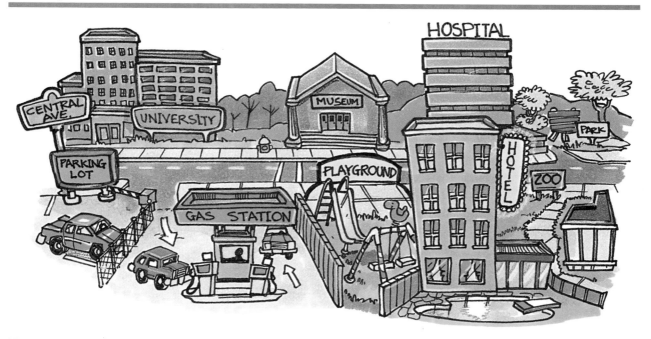

hospital?

A. Excuse me. Could you please tell me how to get to the hospital from here?

B. Sure. **Walk along** Central Avenue and you'll see the hospital **on the left, between** the museum and the park.

A. Thanks.

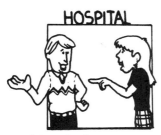

1. *parking lot?*

2. *university?*

3. *park?*

4. *museum?*

5. *playground?*

6. *zoo?*

Would You Please Tell Me How to Get to the Bus Station from Here?

turn right
turn left

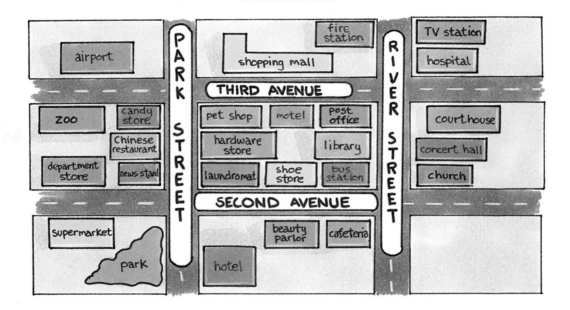

A. Excuse me. Would you please tell me how to get to the bus station from here?

B. Certainly. **Walk up** Park Street to Second Avenue and **turn right.** **Walk along** Second Avenue and you'll see the bus station **on the left, across from** the cafeteria.

A. Thanks very much.

bus station?

A. Excuse me. Would you please tell me how to get to the concert hall from here?

B. Certainly. **Drive along** Second Avenue to River Street and **turn left.** **Drive up** River Street and you'll see the concert hall **on the right, between** the courthouse and the church.

A. Thanks very much.

concert hall?

1. *shopping mall?*

2. *hardware store?*

3. *library?*

4. *zoo?*

5. *department store?*

6. *TV station?*

7. *hospital?*

8.

Take the Main Street Bus and Get Off at First Avenue

A. Excuse me.   What's the quickest way to get to Peter's Pet Shop?

B. **Take** the Main Street bus and **get off** at First Avenue.
Walk up First Avenue and you'll see Peter's Pet Shop **on the right.**

A. Thank you very much.

B. You're welcome.

A. Excuse me.   What's the easiest way to get to Harry's Barber Shop?

B. **Take** the subway and **get off** at Fourth Avenue.
Walk down Fourth Avenue and you'll see Harry's Barber Shop
on the left.

A. Thank you very much.

B. You're welcome.

1. What's the fastest way to get to the baseball stadium?

2. What's the best way to get to St. Andrew's Church?

3. What's the most direct way to get to the zoo?

4. I'm in a hurry!   What's the shortest way to get to the train station?

READING

HAROLD NEVER GOT THERE

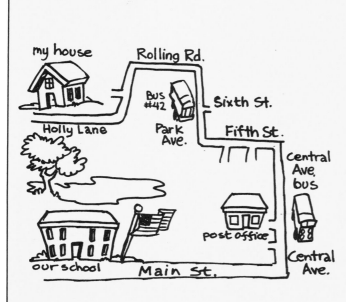

Directions to my house

1. From our school, walk along Main St. to Central Ave. and turn left.
2. Walk up Central Ave. 2 blocks, and you'll see a bus stop at the corner, in front of the post office.
3. Take the Central Ave. bus and get off at Fifth St.
4. Turn left and walk along Fifth St. 3 blocks to Park Ave. and turn right.
5. Walk up Park Ave. 1 block, and you'll see a bus stop at the corner of Park Ave. and Sixth St.
6. Take Bus #42 and get off at Rolling Rd.
7. Turn left and walk along Rolling Rd. 1 block.
8. Turn left again, and walk 2 blocks to Holly Lane and turn right.
9. Walk along Holly Lane. My house is the last one on the right.

Harold had a very difficult time last night. All the other students in his English class went to a party at their teacher's house, but Harold never got there. He followed his teacher's directions, but he made one little mistake.

From their school, he walked along Main Street to Central Avenue and turned left. He walked up Central Avenue two blocks to the bus stop at the corner, in front of the post office. He took the Central Avenue bus and got off at Fifth Street. He turned left and walked along Fifth Street three blocks to Park Avenue and turned right. He walked up Park Avenue one block to the bus stop at the corner of Park Avenue and Sixth Street.

He took Bus Number 42, but he got off at the wrong stop. He got off at River Road instead of Rolling Road. He turned left and walked along River Road one block. He turned left again and walked two blocks, turned right, and got completely lost.

Harold was very upset. He really wanted to go to the party last night, and he can't believe he made such a stupid mistake.

True or False?

1. Harold's English teacher lives on Holly Lane.
2. The Central Avenue bus stops in front of the post office.
3. The teacher made one little mistake in the directions.
4. Harold took the wrong bus.
5. Bus Number 42 goes to Rolling Road.
6. Harold didn't really want to go to the party last night.

What's the Word?

It's very easy to get _____ the zoo from
here.   Walk up this street _____ the corner
and turn right.   Walk two blocks and you'll
see a bus stop _____ the corner _____
Grove Street and Fourth Avenue.   Take the
West Side bus and get _____ _____ Park
Road.   You'll see the zoo _____ the left.   It's
next _____ the library and across _____
the museum.

Listening

I.   Listen and choose the word you hear.

1. a. right   b. left
2. a. down   b. up
3. a. down   b. along
4. a. to   b. on
5. a. of   b. off
6. a. on   b. at

II.   Where is the conversation taking place? Listen and choose.

1. a. pet shop   b. cafeteria
2. a. restaurant   b. library
3. a. department   b. laundromat
      store
4. a. hospital   b. hotel
5. a. beauty parlor   b. supermarket

IN YOUR OWN WORDS

For Writing and Discussion

You're going to invite people to your home.
Draw a map and write directions to help them get
there.   (Give them directions from your school.)

A. Can you recommend **a good hotel?**

B. Yes. The Bellview is **a good hotel.** I think it's **one of the best hotels** in town.

A. Can you tell me how to get there?

B. Sure. Take the subway and get off at Brighton Boulevard. You'll see the Bellview at the corner of Brighton Boulevard and Twelfth Street.

A. Thank you very much.

B. You're welcome.

These people are visiting your city. Using the conversation as a guide, recommend real places you know and like, and give directions.

1.

Can you recommend a good restaurant?

Can you recommend a cheap department store?

2.

3.

Can you recommend a quiet, romantic café?

Can you recommend _____?

4.

SCHOOL CONNECTIONS: The Macintosh Desktop

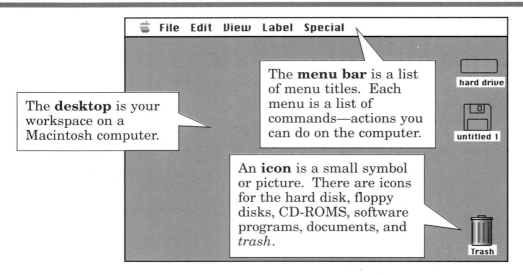

The **desktop** is your workspace on a Macintosh computer.

The **menu bar** is a list of menu titles. Each menu is a list of commands—actions you can do on the computer.

An **icon** is a small symbol or picture. There are icons for the hard disk, floppy disks, CD-ROMS, software programs, documents, and *trash*.

FOLLOWING DIRECTIONS

Select, drag, and open an icon.

Look at the Trash icon on the desktop. What color is it?

Use the mouse or trackball to put the pointer on the icon. Click the icon. What color is it now? You just **selected** the icon.

Now press and hold the button and move the mouse or trackball. What's happening to the icon? Release the button. You just **dragged** the icon.

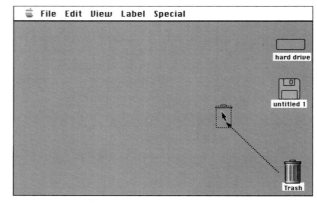

Now double-click on the icon. What do you see? You just **opened** the icon. Now you see a window.

Pull down a menu.

Point to the menu title *File* with the mouse or trackball. Press the mouse or trackball button. What do you see? This is called a **pull-down menu**. It contains commands.

Hold down the button, drag the pointer down the menu, stop at the *Open* command, and release the button. What do you see?

Practice these directions on a computer. Then use the *tutorial* for the computer to learn more about the basic computer skills on this page.

Describing People's
  Actions ■
Performance on the Job
  and in School ■
Describing Plans and
  Intentions ■
Consequences of Actions
Superstitions ■
Understanding Feedback ■

Adverbs ■
Comparatives of
  Adverbs ■
Agent Nouns ■
If-Clauses ■

He Drives Very Carelessly

slow – slowly bad – badly beautiful – beautifully	terrible – terribly miserable – miserably simple – simply	sloppy – sloppily busy – busily lazy – lazily	fast – fast hard – hard good – well

work – a worker
play – a player
drive – a driver

A. I think he's **a careless driver.**

B. I agree.   He **drives VERY carelessly.**

1. *a careless skier*

2. *a slow chess player*

3. *a beautiful singer*

4. *sloppy painters*

5. *an accurate translator*

6. *a good teacher*

7. *careful workers*

8. *a graceful dancer*

9. *good tennis players*

10. *dishonest card players*

11. *a fast driver*

12. *a hard worker*

He Should Try to Speak More Slowly

softly – { more softly / softer }

loud(ly) – { more loudly / louder }

slowly – { more slowly / slower }

neatly – { more neatly / neater }

carefully – more carefully
politely – more politely

hard – harder
fast – faster
early – earlier
late – later

A. Bob speaks VERY **quickly.**

B. You're right. He should try to speak { **more slowly** / **slower** }.

1. Linda speaks very softly.

2. Ronald goes to bed very late.

3. Janet skates very carelessly.

4. Your friends come to class very early.

5. David types very slowly.

6. They dress very sloppily.

7. Peter speaks to his parents very impolitely.

8. Karen plays her record player very loud.

9. They work very slowly.

TRYING HARDER

Michael's boss talked with him today. In general, she doesn't think Michael is doing very well on the job. He has to do better. According to Michael's boss, he types too slowly. He should type faster. In addition, he files too carelessly. He should file more carefully. Furthermore, he speaks on the telephone too quickly. He should speak slower. Michael wants to do well on the job, and he knows now that he has to try a little harder.

Stella's director talked with her today. In general, he doesn't think Stella is doing very well in his play. She has to do better. According to Stella's director, she speaks too softly. She should speak louder. In addition, she walks too slowly. She should walk faster. Furthermore, she dances too awkwardly. She should dance more gracefully. Stella wants to do well in the play, and she knows now that she has to try a little harder.

Billy's teacher talked with him today. In general, she doesn't think Billy is doing very well in school. He has to do better. According to Billy's teacher, he arrives at school too late. He should arrive earlier. In addition, he dresses too sloppily. He should dress neater. Furthermore, he speaks too impolitely. He should speak more politely. Billy wants to do well in school, and he knows now that he has to try a little harder.

✓CHECK-UP

Q & A

Michael is talking with his boss. Stella is talking with her director. Billy is talking with his teacher. Using this model, create dialogs based on the story.

A. Do I *type fast* enough?
B. No. You *type* too *slowly*.
A. Oh. I'll try to *type faster* in the future.

Opposites

1. earlier _____*later*_____
2. faster _____
3. politely _____
4. carefully _____
5. sloppily _____
6. quietly _____
7. awkwardly _____

68

If

If _____ will _____

A. What are they going to name their new baby?

B. If they have a boy, they'll name him John. If they have a girl, they'll name her Jane.

1. A. How are you going to get to school tomorrow?

   B. If it rains, I'll _____.
   If it's sunny, I'll _____.

2. A. What's Bob going to do this Saturday afternoon?

   B. If the weather is good, he'll _____.
   If the weather is bad, he'll _____.

3. A. What's Carmen going to have for dinner tonight?

   B. If she's very hungry, _____.
   If she isn't very hungry, _____.

4. A. What's Fred going to do tomorrow?

   B. If he feels better, _____.
   If he doesn't feel better, _____.

5. A. When are you going to go to sleep tonight?

   B. If I'm tired, _____.
   If I'm not tired, _____.

6. A. What are they going to wear tomorrow?

   B. If it's hot, _____.
   If it's cool, _____.

How about YOU?

What are you going to do tonight if you have a lot of homework?
What are you going to do tonight if you DON'T have a lot of homework?

What are you going to have for breakfast tomorrow if you're very hungry?
What are you going to have for breakfast tomorrow if you AREN'T very hungry?

What are you going to do this weekend if the weather is nice?
What are you going to do this weekend if the weather is bad?

If You Drive Too Fast, You Might Have an Accident

If _____ might _____

A. You know . . . you shouldn't drive so fast.

B. Oh?

A. Yes.   If you drive too fast, you might have an accident.

B. Hmm.   You're probably right.

1. *work so slowly*
   lose your job

2. *sing so loud*
   get a sore throat

3. *worry so much*
   get an ulcer

4. *eat so much candy*
   get a toothache

5. *do your homework so*
   carelessly
   make too many mistakes

6. *go to bed so late*
   be tired in the
   morning

7. *use those headphones*
   so often
   hurt your ears

8. *watch so many scary*
   TV programs
   have nightmares

9.

TOO BAD!

Ronald wants to stay up late to watch a movie tonight, but he knows he shouldn't. If he stays up late to watch a movie, he won't get to bed until after midnight. If he doesn't get to bed until after midnight, he'll probably be very tired in the morning. If he's very tired in the morning, he might oversleep. If he oversleeps, he'll be late for work. If he's late for work, his boss might get angry and fire him. So, even though Ronald wants to stay up late to watch a movie tonight, he isn't going to. Too bad!

Barbara wants to buy a new car, but she knows she shouldn't. If she buys a new car, she'll have to take a lot of money out of her bank account. If she has to take a lot of money out of her bank account, she won't have much left. If she doesn't have much left, she won't have enough to pay the rent. If she doesn't have enough to pay the rent, her landlord might evict her from her apartment. So, even though Barbara wants to buy a new car, she isn't going to. Too bad!

Mr. and Mrs. Watson want to move to Arizona, but they know they shouldn't. If they move to Arizona, they'll be far away from their children and grandchildren in New Jersey. If they're far away from their children and grandchildren in New Jersey, they won't see them very often. If they don't see them very often, they'll feel lonely and depressed. So, even though Mr. and Mrs. Watson want to move to Arizona, they aren't going to. Too bad!

✓ CHECK-UP

Choose

1. If Ronald _____ go to bed early, he'll be tired in the morning.
   a. doesn't
   b. won't

2. His boss might fire him if _____ late for work.
   a. he'll be
   b. he's

3. Barbara _____ a lot of money if she buys a new car.
   a. spends
   b. will spend

4. If Barbara _____ pay the rent, her landlord might evict her.
   a. can't
   b. won't

5. If Mr. and Mrs. Watson move, they _____ see their family very often.
   a. don't
   b. won't

6. The Watsons won't feel lonely if they _____ move.
   a. don't
   b. might not

Complete These Sentences

1. If I stay up late tonight, . . .
2. If it rains tomorrow, . . .
3. If I'm not busy on Saturday, . . .
4. If the weather is nice on Sunday, . . .
5. If I don't practice English, . . .

Listening

Listen and choose the best answer to complete the sentence.

1. a. he'll be tired tomorrow.
   b. he'll be early in the future.

2. a. her boss might fire her.
   b. her landlord might evict her.

3. a. their grandchildren will move to New Jersey.
   b. their grandchildren will be far away.

4. a. my teacher will be happy.
   b. my teacher won't be happy.

5. a. he won't go back to school.
   b. he'll go back to school.

6. a. his train won't arrive on time.
   b. he might lose his job.

 IN YOUR OWN WORDS

For Writing and Discussion

Tell about something you want to do but you know you shouldn't. For example:

"I want to stop studying English."
"I want to move to _____."
"I want to buy an expensive _____."

TOO BAD

I want to _____, but I know I shouldn't. If _____, _____. If _____, _____. If . . .
.
.
So, even though I want to _____, I'm not going to. Too bad!

ON YOUR OWN: Superstitions

Many people believe that you'll have GOOD luck

    if you find a four-leaf clover.
    if you find a horseshoe.
    if you give a new pair of shoes to a poor person.

You'll have BAD luck

    if a black cat walks in front of you.
    if you walk under a ladder.
    if you open an umbrella in your house.
    if you put your shoes on a table.

Here are some other superstitions.

If your right eye itches, you'll laugh soon.
If your left eye itches, you'll cry soon.

If your right ear itches, somebody is saying good things about you.
If your left ear itches, somebody is saying bad things about you.

If a knife falls, a man will visit soon.
If a fork falls, a woman will visit soon.
If a spoon falls, a baby will visit soon.

If you break a mirror, you'll have bad luck for seven years.

If you spill salt, you should throw a little salt over your left shoulder.
If you don't, you'll have bad luck.

Do you know any superstitions? Share them with other students in your class.

73

SCHOOL CONNECTIONS: Understanding Feedback

These school personnel are giving students feedback. What are they saying?
Fill in the missing words.

1. You're talking too loud. Please talk _more quietly_ .

2. You're running too slowly. Try to run _____.

3. You're late again! You have to get here _____.

4. You're taking the test too carelessly. You should check your answers _____.

5. You're talking to your teachers very impolitely. Please speak to them _____.

6. You're playing too fast. Let's try it again _____.

What kind of feedback do you hear at school? Write the sentences you hear.
Then share them with your classmates.

9

Describing Ongoing Past
    Activities ■
Reporting a Crime ■
Expressing Regret ■
Telling about an
    Accident ■
Mishaps
Conflict Resolution ■

Past Continuous Tense ■
Reflexive Pronouns ■
While-Clauses ■

The Blackout

| I He She It | was | working. |
| We You They | were | |

Last night at 8:00 there was a blackout in Centerville.   The lights went out all over town.

A. What was Doris doing last night when the lights went out?

B. She was taking a bath.

A. What were Mr. and Mrs. Green doing last night when the lights went out?

B. They were riding in an elevator.

Ask about these people.

1. *Ted*

2. *Irene*

3. *Bob and Judy*

4. *you*

5. *Joe*

6. *your parents*

7. *your younger sister*

8. *your father*

9. *Mr. and Mrs. Jones*

What were YOU doing last night at 8:00?

76

I Saw You Yesterday, but You Didn't See Me

A. I saw you yesterday, but you didn't see me.

B. Really? When?

A. At about 2:30. You were **getting out of a taxi on Main Street.**

B. That wasn't me. Yesterday at 2:30 I was **cooking dinner.**

A. Hmm. I guess I made a mistake.

1. *walking into the post office*
fixing my car

3. *getting on a bus*
watching TV

5. *jogging through the park*
playing tennis

7. *getting out of a police car*
sleeping

2. *walking out of the laundromat*
cleaning my apartment

4. *getting off a merry-go-round*
playing baseball

6. *riding your bicycle along Main Street*
cooking

8.

A ROBBERY

There was a robbery at 151 River Street yesterday afternoon. Burglars broke into every apartment in the building while all the tenants were out.

The man in Apartment 1 wasn't home. He was washing his clothes at the laundromat. The woman in Apartment 2 wasn't home either. She was visiting a friend in the hospital. The people in Apartment 3 were gone. They were having a picnic at the beach. The man in Apartment 4 was out. He was playing tennis in the park. The college students in Apartment 5 were away. They were attending a football game. And the elderly lady in Apartment 6 was out of town. She was visiting her grandchildren in Ohio.

Yesterday certainly was an unfortunate day for the people at 151 River Street. They had no idea that while they were away, burglars broke into every apartment in the building.

CHECK-UP

Q & A

The tenants at 151 River Street are talking to the police. Using this model, create dialogs based on the story.

A. Which apartment do you live in?
B. Apartment *1*.
A. Were you home at the time of the robbery?
B. No, I wasn't. I was *washing my clothes at the laundromat.*
A. What did the burglars take from your apartment?
B. They took my *stereo*, my *computer*, and some money I had in *a drawer in my bedroom.*
A. How much?
B. About *three hundred dollars*.

He Went to the Movies by Himself

I	myself
you	yourself
he	himself
she	herself
it	itself
we	ourselves
you	yourselves
they	themselves

A. What did **John** do yesterday?

B. He went to the movies.

A. Oh.   Who did he go to the movies with?

B. Nobody.   He went to the movies **by himself.**

1. *Patty*
   go to the beach

2. *Peter*
   go to the ballgame

3. *you*
   go bowling

4. *you and your wife*
   play cards

5. *Susan and Robert*
   have a picnic

6. *you*
   go to Bob's party

7. *Mrs. Wilson*
   drive to New York

8. *Mr. Wilson*
   take a walk in the park.

9.

I Had a Bad Day Today

A. You look upset.

B. I had a bad day today.

A. Why? What happened?

B. I **lost my wallet** while I was **jogging through the park.**

A. I'm sorry to hear that.*

A. Harry looks upset.

B. He had a bad day today.

A. Why? What happened?

B. He **cut himself** while he was **shaving.**

A. That's too bad.*

*Or: How awful! That's terrible! What a shame! What a pity!

1. *you*

   burned myself cooking dinner

2. *Sheila*

   dropped her packages walking out of the supermarket

3. *Tom*

   hurt himself playing basketball

4. your parents

got a flat tire
driving over a bridge

5. you

fainted
waiting for the bus

6. Nelson

saw a few gray hairs
looking at himself in
the mirror

7. you and your wife

had an accident
driving home

8. Linda

cut herself
slicing a tomato

9. you

a dog bit me
standing on the corner

10. Marvin

tripped and fell
walking to work

11. your aunt and uncle

somebody stole their car
shopping

12. you

a can of paint fell on me
walking under a ladder

How about YOU?

Everybody has a bad day once in a while. Try
to remember a few days when something bad
happened to you. What happened, and what were
you doing when it happened?

FRIDAY THE 13TH

Yesterday was Friday the 13th.   Many people believe that Friday the 13th is a very unlucky day.   I, myself, didn't think so . . . until yesterday.

Yesterday I cut myself while I was shaving.

My wife burned herself while she was cooking breakfast.

My son poked himself in the eye while he was putting on his glasses.

Our daughter spilled soup all over herself while she was eating dinner.

Both our children hurt themselves while they were playing outside.

And we all got wet paint all over ourselves while we were sitting in the park across the street.

I'm not usually superstitious, but yesterday was a VERY unlucky day.   So, the next time it's Friday the 13th, do yourself a favor!   Take care of yourself!

 CHECK-UP

Q & A

The man in the story is talking with a friend. Using this model, create dialogs based on the story.

A.   *My wife* had a bad day yesterday.
B.   Oh?   What happened?
A.   *She burned herself* while *she was cooking breakfast.*
B.   That's too bad.

How about YOU?

Are you superstitious?   Do you believe that certain days are lucky or unlucky?   Which days, and why?

What's the Word?

1. She spilled the _____.
   a. juice   b. children   c. dog

2. I lost my _____.
   a. park   b. accident   c. purse

3. He poked himself in the _____.
   a. gray hair   b. eye   c. glasses

4. They tripped and _____.
   a. dropped   b. fell   c. shaved

5. I was slicing a _____.
   a. flat tire   b. cut   c. banana

6. What a _____!
   a. sorry   b. bad   c. pity

Listening

Listen to the conversations. What happened to these people? Listen and choose the best answer.

1. a. He cut himself.
   b. He looked at himself.

2. a. She tripped.
   b. She got a flat tire.

3. a. They hurt themselves in the basement.
   b. They fell down in the yard.

4. a. He burned himself.
   b. He fainted.

5. a. Somebody stole his wallet.
   b. He got paint on his pants.

READING

AN ACCIDENT

I saw an accident this morning while I was standing at the corner of Elm Street and Central Avenue. A woman in a small red sports car was driving very quickly down Elm Street. A man in a large green truck was driving along Central Avenue very slowly. While he was driving through the intersection, the woman in the red sports car didn't stop at a stop sign and she crashed into the truck. Fortunately, the woman wasn't hurt, but her nose was bleeding a little. The man in the truck wasn't hurt at all. He was shouting at the lady. I left when the police came. I'm glad nobody was hurt very badly.

✓ CHECK-UP

True, False, or Maybe?

Answer True, False, or Maybe (if the answer isn't in the story).

1. The accident took place at the corner of Elm Street and Central Avenue.
2. The woman was driving a small green sports car.
3. The truck driver is always very careful.
4. The truck crashed into the sports car.
5. The woman didn't see the stop sign.
6. The police came after the accident.
7. The woman was tired.

How about YOU?

Tell about an accident you saw:
    Where were you? What happened?
    Was anybody hurt?

SCHOOL CONNECTIONS: Conflict Resolution

A. All right, you two. Stop it! No fighting! Now, what's going on?

B. She punched me.

C. Yeah, I punched him.

A. Why?

C. He was bothering me.

A. What was he doing?

C. He was making faces at me.

B. That's not true. I wasn't making faces at her. She was calling me names.

C. No, I wasn't.

B. Yes, you were.

A. Cool it! Both of you. Let's continue this conversation in the assistant principal's office.

B. Oh, brother!

C. Now we're in trouble! Ms. Taylor, we're okay. We were just having a little disagreement.

A. You were fighting. That's against the school rules. You know that. Now let's go.

These students are having a conflict. Why? What do you think is going to happen next? Work with a group of students. Role-play the conversation in the assistant principal's office. Perform your role play for the class.

Do students sometimes argue or fight in your school? About what? What happens to students when they get into fights?

How do you think students, teachers, and schools can prevent fights in schools? Make a list of suggestions:

_____

_____

_____

Does your school have a **conflict resolution** program? If it does, talk in class about how this program works.

Expressing Past and Future
   Ability ■

Expressing Past and Future
   Obligation ■

Making Excuses ■

Repair Services ■

Telling about Frustrations and
   Disappointments ■

Giving Explanations and
   Making Excuses ■

Could ■
Be Able to ■
Have Got to ■
Too + Adjectives ■

They Couldn't

I	
He	
She	
It	could/couldn't study.
We	
You	
They	

Could he study?
Yes, he could.
No, he couldn't.

A. Could Peter play on the basketball team when he was a little boy?

B. No, he couldn't. He was too **short**.

1. Could Henry go to work yesterday?
sick

2. Could Rita go out with her boyfriend last weekend?
busy

3. Could Mr. and Mrs. Jones finish their dinner?
full

4. Could Billy get into the movie last Saturday night?
young

5. Could you finish your homework last night?
tired

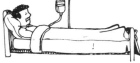

6. Could Frank get out of bed the day after his operation?
weak

7. Could Betty tell the policeman about her accident?
upset

8. Could Stuart eat at his wedding?
nervous

86

They Weren't Able to

could $= \begin{Bmatrix} \text{was} \\ \text{were} \end{Bmatrix}$ able to

couldn't $= \begin{Bmatrix} \text{wasn't} \\ \text{weren't} \end{Bmatrix}$ able to

A. Was Jimmy able to lift his grandmother's suitcase?

B. No, he wasn't able to. It was too **heavy.**

1. Was Louise able to paint her house yesterday afternoon?

   windy

3. Were Mr. and Mrs. Johnson able to go swimming in the ocean during their vacation?

   cold

5. Was Tom able to find his wallet last night?

   dark

7. Were Jeff and Gloria able to see the full moon last night?

   cloudy

2. Was Carl able to sit down on the bus this morning?

   crowded

4. Was Shirley able to finish her order of spaghetti and meatballs?

   spicy

6. Were you able to do the grammar exercises last night?

   difficult

8. Was Willy able to wear his brother's suit to the dance last Saturday night?

   small

She Had to Study for an Examination

A. Did Barbara enjoy herself at the concert last night?

B. Unfortunately, she $\begin{Bmatrix} \text{wasn't able to} \\ \text{couldn't} \end{Bmatrix}$ go to the concert last night.   She had to **study for an examination.**

1. Did Ronald enjoy himself at the baseball game yesterday?

go to the dentist

2. Did you enjoy yourself at the tennis match last week?

visit my boss in the hospital

3. Did Mr. and Mrs. Wilson enjoy themselves at the symphony yesterday evening?

wait for the plumber

4. Did Sally enjoy herself at the theater last Saturday night?

take care of her little brother

5. Did Fred enjoy himself at Mary's party last Friday evening?

work late at the office

6. Did you and your classmates enjoy yourselves at the movies last night?

study English

7. Did Marion enjoy herself at the picnic last Sunday?

take care of her neighbor's dog

8. Did you enjoy yourself at the football game yesterday?

fix a flat tire

9. _____

READING

MRS. MURPHY'S STUDENTS COULDN'T DO THEIR HOMEWORK

Mrs. Murphy doesn't know what to do with her students today. They didn't do their homework last night, and now she can't teach the lesson she prepared.

Bob couldn't do his homework because he had a stomachache. Sally couldn't do her homework because she was tired and fell asleep early. John couldn't do his homework because he had to visit his grandmother in the hospital. Donna couldn't do her homework because she had to take care of her baby sister while her mother worked late at the office. And all the other students couldn't do their homework because there was a blackout in their neighborhood last night.

All the students promise Mrs. Murphy they'll be able to do their homework tonight. She certainly hopes so.

 CHECK-UP

Q & A

Mrs. Murphy is asking her students about their homework. Using this model, create dialogs based on the story.

A. *Bob?* Where's your homework?
B. I'm sorry, Mrs. Murphy. I couldn't do it.
A. You couldn't? Why not?
B. *I had a stomachache.*
A. Will you do your homework tonight?
B. Yes. I promise.

Choose

What word *doesn't* belong?

1.	a.	upset	b.	nervous	c.	tired	d.	crowded
2.	a.	brother	b.	plumber	c.	teacher	d.	dentist
3.	a.	windy	b.	cold	c.	cloudy	d.	dark
4.	a.	nervous	b.	hungry	c.	thirsty	d.	full
5.	a.	movie	b.	match	c.	wedding	d.	concert

Listening

Listen and choose the best answer.

1. a. It was too crowded.
   b. It was too noisy.

2. a. It was too windy.
   b. It was too cloudy.

3. a. No. It was too full.
   b. No. It was very spicy.

4. a. He was too weak.
   b. He was too heavy.

5. a. They were busy.
   b. They were difficult.

I'm Afraid I Won't Be Able to Help You

will/won't be able to

I've We've You've They've } got to = I We You They } have to	work.

He's She's It's } got to = He She It } has to

A. I'm afraid I won't be able to help you **move to your new apartment** tomorrow.

B. You won't?   Why not?

A. I've got to **take my son to the doctor.**

B. Don't worry about it!   I'm sure I'll be able to **move to my new apartment** by myself.

1. *clean your garage*
   go to the office

2. *paint your living room*
   fly to Chicago

3. *fix your car*
   drive my husband to the clinic

4. *do your homework*
   practice the piano

5. *repair your kitchen window*
   take care of my neighbor's baby

6. *cook Christmas dinner*
   buy presents for my children

7. *study for the examination*
   take my sister to her ballet lesson

8. *take Jennifer to the dentist*
   work overtime at the factory

9. *take Rover to the vet*
   visit my mother in the hospital

10.

READING

THE BATHROOM PIPE IS BROKEN

Mr. and Mrs. Wilson are very frustrated. A pipe broke in their bathroom yesterday while Mr. Wilson was taking a shower. They called the plumber, but she couldn't come yesterday. She was sick. She can't come today either. She's too busy. And, unfortunately, she won't be able to come tomorrow because tomorrow is Sunday, and she doesn't work on Sundays. Mr. and Mrs. Wilson are afraid they won't be able to use their shower for quite a while. That's why they're so frustrated.

THE TELEVISION IS BROKEN

Timmy Brown and all his brothers and sisters are very frustrated. Their television broke yesterday while they were watching their favorite TV program. Their parents called the TV repairman, but he couldn't come yesterday. He was fixing televisions on the other side of town. He can't come today either. His repair truck is broken. And, unfortunately, he won't be able to come tomorrow because he'll be out of town. Timmy Brown and all his brothers and sisters are afraid they won't be able to watch TV for quite a while. That's why they're so frustrated.

✔ CHECK-UP

Answer These Questions

1. Could the plumber come to the Wilsons' house yesterday? Why not?
2. Can she come to their house today? Why not?
3. Will she be able to come to their house tomorrow? Why not?

4. Could the TV repairman come to the Browns' house yesterday? Why not?
5. Can he come to their house today? Why not?
6. Will he be able to come to their house tomorrow? Why not?

Choose

Mr. Wilson is calling the plumber. Choose the correct words and then practice the conversation.

A. Hello. This is Mr. Wilson again. You [have to / got to]¹ send someone over here to fix

our bathroom pipe. I've [have to / got to]² take a shower!

B. I'm sorry, Mr. Wilson. You've [have to / got to]³ understand. We [can't / aren't]⁴ able to

send a plumber right now. I [have to / have]⁵ a big job to do on the other side of town

and my assistant [has / has to]⁶ got to help me. We won't [can't / be able to]⁷ come

over for a few more days.

92

1. George is upset. He got a flat tire, and he won't be able to get to the airport on time.

2. Rita is frustrated. She lost her key, and she can't get into her apartment.

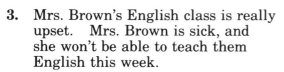

3. Mrs. Brown's English class is really upset. Mrs. Brown is sick, and she won't be able to teach them English this week.

4. Sidney is disappointed. He wasn't able to find a job in New York City, and he had to move home with his mother and father.

5. Ted was really disappointed last year. He couldn't dance in the school play. His teacher said he was too clumsy.

Are you frustrated, disappointed, or upset about something? Tell the class about your problem. If you don't have a problem now, tell the class about the LAST time you were frustrated, disappointed, or upset.

SCHOOL CONNECTIONS: Giving Explanations and Making Excuses

A. I couldn't do my homework last night.

B. Why not?

A. I was very sick.

B. I see. Well, do it tonight and I'll correct it tomorrow.

A. Okay. Thank you.

A. I wasn't able to do my homework last night.

B. Why not?

A. Our basketball game ended late, and then we all went out for pizza.

B. That's no excuse. You have to make time for your homework. I expect to see it tomorrow.

A. All right.

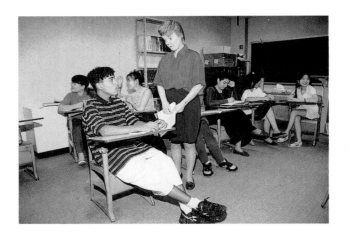

Sometimes students don't do their homework. There are good excuses, and there are bad excuses. With a partner, brainstorm five good excuses and five bad excuses. Then share as a class. Make two complete lists of excuses and discuss them.

Good Excuses	Bad Excuses
1. _____	1. _____
2. _____	2. _____
3. _____	3. _____
4. _____	4. _____
5. _____	5. _____

With another partner, practice two role plays between teachers and students. In one conversation, the student has a good excuse. In the other conversation, the student has a bad excuse. Perform your role plays for the class.

Health ■
Nutrition ■
Following Instructions ■
Medical Examinations ■
Medical Advice ■
Home Remedies ■
School Rules ■

Must ■
Must vs. Should ■
Count/Non-Count
  Nouns ■
Past Tense Review ■

Diets

I He She It We You They } must work.

more/less	more/fewer
bread	cookies
fish	potatoes
fruit	eggs

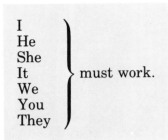

Henry's Diet	
⊖	⊕
bread	fish
cookies	vegetables
candy	fruit
potato chips	
other snack foods	

1. Henry had his yearly checkup today. The doctor told him he's a little too heavy and put him on this diet:

   He must eat **less** bread, **fewer** cookies, **less** candy, and **fewer** potato chips and other snack foods.

   Also, he must eat **more** fish, **more** vegetables, and **more** fruit.

Shirley's Diet	
⊖	⊕
fatty meat	lean meat
potatoes	grapefruit
rice	green vegetables
rich desserts	

2. Shirley also had her annual checkup today. Her doctor put her on this diet:

   She must eat _____

   _____

   _____

Arthur's Diet	
⊖	⊕
butter	margarine
eggs	skim milk
cheese	yogurt
ice cream	

3. Arthur was worried about his heart.   He went to his doctor for an examination, and the doctor told him to eat fewer fatty foods.

He must eat/drink _____

_____

_____

Rover's Diet	
⊖	⊕
fatty meat	lean meat
dog biscuits	water

4. Rover went to the vet yesterday for his yearly checkup.   The vet told him he's a little too heavy and put him on this diet:

He must eat/drink _____

_____

_____

My Diet	
⊖	⊕

5. You went to the doctor today for your annual physical examination. The doctor told you you're a little overweight and said you must go on a diet.

I must eat/drink _____

_____

_____

CAROL'S APPLE CAKE

Carol baked an apple cake yesterday, but she couldn't follow all the instructions in her cookbook because she didn't have enough of the ingredients. She used less flour and fewer eggs than the recipe required. She also used less butter, fewer apples, fewer raisins, and less sugar than she was supposed to. As a result, Carol's apple cake didn't taste very good. As a matter of fact, it tasted terrible!

PAUL'S BEEF STEW

Paul cooked beef stew yesterday, but he couldn't follow all the instructions in his cookbook because he didn't have enough of the ingredients. He used less meat and fewer tomatoes than the recipe required. He also used fewer potatoes, less salt, less red wine, and fewer onions than he was supposed to. As a result, Paul's beef stew didn't taste very good. As a matter of fact, it tasted awful!

✔ CHECK-UP

What's the Word?

Steve and Judy built their own house last year, but they couldn't follow the blueprints exactly because they didn't have enough money to buy all the construction materials they needed. They used _____ wood
1
and _____ nails than the blueprints
2
required. They also used _____
3
cement, _____ pipes, _____
4 5
electrical wiring, and _____ bricks than
6
they were supposed to. As a result, their house didn't last very long. As a matter of fact, it fell down last week!

Listening

Listen and choose the best words to complete the sentences.

1.	a.	eggs	b.	salt	4. a. strawberries	b.	butter
2.	a.	raisins	b.	flour	5. a. onions	b.	cheese
3.	a.	potatoes	b.	rice	6. a. hamburgers	b.	food

I Must Lose Some Weight

must/mustn't (must not)

A. I had my yearly checkup today.

B. What did the doctor say?

A. He/She told me I'm a little too heavy and I must lose some weight.

B. Do you have to stop eating _____?

A. No, but I mustn't eat as (much/many)_____ as I did before.

1.

2.

3.

4.

5.

6.

7.

8.

9.

The Checkup

Hello, Roger.   Maybe you can help me.
I want to get a medical checkup, but my doctor moved away.

You should go to MY doctor . . . Dr. Anderson.
He'll give you a very complete examination.

1.  The nurse will lead you into one of the examination rooms.

2.  You'll stand on a scale so the nurse can measure your height and your weight.

3.  The nurse will leave, and you'll take off your clothes and put on a hospital gown.

4.  Dr. Anderson will come in, shake your hand, and say "hello."

5.  First, he'll examine your eyes, ears, nose, and throat.

6.  Then, he'll listen to your heart with a stethoscope.

7.  Next, he'll take your pulse.

8.  Then, he'll take your blood pressure.

9.  After that, he'll draw some blood for a blood test.

10.  Finally, he'll take a chest X-ray and do a cardiogram.

Your Checkup

You had a complete physical examination yesterday. Tell us about your visit to the doctor.

1. The nurse **led** me _____.

2. _____.

3. _____.

4. _____.

5. _____.

6. _____.

7. _____.

8. _____.

9. _____.

10. _____.

Really, Doctor?

A. I'm really worried about your heart.

B. Really, Doctor?   Should I stop eating rich desserts?

A. Mr. Jones!   You MUST stop eating rich desserts!   If you don't, you're going to have serious problems with your heart some day.

A. I'm really worried about your _____.

B. Really, Doctor?   Should I _____?

A. (Mr./Miss/Mrs./Ms.) _____!   You MUST _____!
If you don't, you're going to have serious problems with
your _____ some day.

1. *lungs*
   stop smoking

2. *back*
   start doing exercises

3. *feet*
   stop jogging

4. *blood pressure*
   take life a little easier

5. *hearing*
   stop listening to loud
   rock music

6.

ON YOUR OWN: Home Remedies

What do YOU do when you burn your finger?

Some people rub butter on their finger.

Other people put a piece of ice on their finger.

Other people put their finger under cold water.

Different people have different remedies for medical problems that aren't very serious. The following people need your advice. Help them with their medical problems and share your "home remedies" with the other students in your class.

1. I have a cold. What should I do?

2. I have a toothache. What should I do?

3. I have a stomachache. What should I do?

4. I have a bloody nose. What should I do?

5. I have the hiccups. What should I do?

Students MUST . . .
- stay on school grounds during the lunch period
- have a hall pass to walk in the halls during class time
- act respectfully toward each other

Students MUSTN'T . . .
- run in the halls
- go to their lockers between classes
- smoke on school grounds
- have drugs or alcohol on school grounds
- use foul language
- fight
- bring beepers or cellular phones to school
- bring weapons into the building
- wear shorts or skirts too high above the knee
- wear form-fitting pants or leggings
- wear shirts with foul language or references to drugs
- wear hats
- bully or threaten other students

Does your school have a student guide with a list of rules? As a class, study the student guide. What rules do you find?

In your school, what happens to students when they break a rule? Do students get *detention*? Where do they *serve* detention? When?

Which school rules do you agree with? Which rules should change? Why?

Describing Future Activities ■
Making Plans by Telephone ■
Expressing Time and
    Duration ■
Holidays ■
Stages of Life ■
Planning Course Selection with
    the Guidance Counselor ■

Future Continuous
Tense ■
Time Expressions ■

Will They Be Home This Evening?

(I will)	I'll
(He will)	He'll
(She will)	She'll
(It will)	It'll
(We will)	We'll
(You will)	You'll
(They will)	They'll

} be working.

A. Will you be home this evening?

B. Yes, I will.   I'll be reading.

1. *Sharon*

2. *Steven*

3. *Mr. and Mrs. Williams*

4. *Bob*

5. *you*

6. *Kathy*

7. *Jack*

8. *you*

9. *Mrs. McDonald*

10. *you and your brother*

11. *Dave*

12. *you*

Hi, Gloria. This Is Arthur.

A. Hi, Gloria. This is Arthur.
Can I come over and visit this evening?

B. No, Arthur. I'm afraid I won't be home this evening. I'll be shopping at the supermarket.

A. Oh. Can I come over and visit TOMORROW evening?

B. No, Arthur. I'm afraid I won't be home tomorrow evening. I'll be working late at the office.

A. I see. Can I come over and visit this WEEKEND?

B. No, Arthur. I'll be visiting my sister in New York.

A. Oh. Well, can I come over and visit next Wednesday?

B. No, Arthur. I'll be visiting my uncle in the hospital.

A. How about sometime next SPRING?

B. No, Arthur. I'll be getting married next spring.

A. Oh!!

B. Good-bye.

When Can You Come Over?

Complete this conversation and practice with another student.

I'm having some problems with the homework for tomorrow.

I'll be glad to help.
When can you come over?

I can come over at _____ o'clock.
Is that okay?

I'm afraid I won't be home at _____ o'clock.
I'll be _____ing.   How about _____ o'clock?

No, I won't be able to come over at _____ o'clock.
I'll be _____ing.   How about _____ o'clock?

Fine.   I'll see you then.

How Long Will Your Aunt Gertrude Be Staying with Us?

A. How long will your Aunt Gertrude be staying with us?

B. She'll be staying with us **for a few months.**

1. How long will they be staying in San Francisco?
   until Friday

3. How late will your husband be working tonight?
   until 10 o'clock

5. How much longer will you be practicing the piano?
   for a few more minutes

7. When will we be arriving in London?
   at 7 A.M.

9. How far will we be driving today?
   until we reach Detroit

2. How much longer will you be working on my car?
   for a few more hours

4. Where will you be getting off?
   at the last stop

6. How late will your daughter be studying this evening?
   until 8 o'clock

8. How much longer will you be reading?
   until I finish this chapter

10. How soon will Santa Claus be coming?
    in a few days

HAPPY THANKSGIVING!

Thanksgiving is this week, and several of our relatives from out of town will be staying with us during the long holiday weekend. Uncle Frank will be staying for a few days. He'll be sleeping on the couch in the living room. Grandma and Grandpa will be staying until next Monday. They'll be sleeping in the guest room over the garage. Cousin Bertha will be staying for a week or more. She'll be sleeping on a cot in the children's bedroom.

My wife and I will be busy for the next few days. She'll be preparing Thanksgiving dinner, and I'll be cleaning the house from top to bottom. We're looking forward to the holiday, but we know we'll be happy when it's over.

Happy Thanksgiving!

CHECK-UP

Q & A

Uncle Frank, Grandma, Grandpa, and Cousin Bertha are calling to ask about the plans for Thanksgiving. Using this model, create dialogs based on the story.

A. Hi! This is *Uncle Frank*!
B. Hi, *Uncle Frank*! How are you?
A. Fine!
B. We're looking forward to seeing you for Thanksgiving.
A. Actually, that's why I'm calling. Are you sure there will be enough room for me?
B. Don't worry! We'll have plenty of room. You'll be sleeping *on the couch in the living room*. Will that be okay?
A. That'll be fine.
B. By the way, *Uncle Frank*, how long will you be staying with us?
A. *For a few days*.
B. That's great! We're really looking forward to seeing you.

What holiday is very special in your family?
How do you celebrate it?

Will You Be Home Today at About Five O'Clock?

A. Hello, Richard.   This is Julie.   I want to return the tennis racket I borrowed from you last week.   Will you be home today at about five o'clock?

B. Yes, I will.   I'll be cooking dinner.

A. Oh.   Then I won't come over at five.

B. Why not?

A. I don't want to disturb you.   You'll be cooking dinner!

B. Don't worry.   You won't disturb me.

A. Okay.   See you at five.

A. Hello, _____. This is _____. I want to return the _____ I borrowed from you last week. Will you be home today at about _____ o'clock?

B. Yes, I will. I'll be _____ing.

A. Oh. Then I won't come over at _____.

B. Why not?

A. I don't want to disturb you. You'll be _____ing!

B. Don't worry. You won't disturb me.

A. Okay. See you at _____.

1. *dictionary*
   doing the laundry

2. *videotape*
   watching my favorite TV program

3. *hammer*
   helping my son with his homework

4. *coffee pot*
   knitting

5. *football*
   ironing

6.

112

GROWING UP

Jessica is growing up. Very soon she'll be walking, she'll be talking, and she'll be playing with the other children in the neighborhood. Jessica can't believe how quickly time flies! She won't be a baby very much longer. Soon she'll be a little girl.

Tommy is growing up. Very soon he'll be shaving, he'll be driving, and he'll be going out on dates. Tommy can't believe how quickly time flies! He won't be a little boy very much longer. Soon he'll be a teenager.

Kathy is growing up. Very soon she'll be going to college, she'll be living away from home, and she'll be starting a career. Kathy can't believe how quickly time flies! She won't be a teenager very much longer. Soon she'll be a young adult.

Peter and Sally are getting older. Very soon they'll be getting married, they'll be having children, and they'll be buying a house. Peter and Sally can't believe how quickly time flies! They won't be young adults very much longer. Soon they'll be middle-aged.

Walter is getting older. Very soon he'll be reaching the age of sixty-five, he'll be retiring, and he'll be taking it easy for the first time in his life. Walter can't believe how quickly time flies! He won't be middle-aged very much longer. Soon he'll be a senior citizen.

CHECK-UP

Listening

Listen and choose the best answer.

1. a. For a few hours.
   b. In a few hours.

2. a. Very soon.
   b. Last Saturday.

3. a. Until 8 o'clock.
   b. For 8 hours.

4. a. In 10 more minutes.
   b. For 10 more minutes.

5. a. Yes. At 9 o'clock.
   b. Yes. Until 9 o'clock.

6. a. Until he stopped working here.
   b. Next year.

How about YOU?

What do you think you'll be doing ten years from now? Tell about your future.

SCHOOL CONNECTIONS: Planning Course Selection with the Guidance Counselor

A. Tell me, Alma, what are your career goals?

B. My career goals?

A. Yes—your long-range plans. What do you think you'll be doing ten years from now?

B. Oh. Now I understand. I think I'll be working as a scientist.

A. Interesting. And what do you think you'll be doing as a scientist?

B. I'm not sure. Maybe I'll be studying pollution and other problems with the environment.

A. Do you think you'll be using mathematics?

B. Probably.

A. Then may I make a suggestion?

B. Sure.

A. I don't think you should take General Mathematics next year. I think you should take Algebra.

B. Oh?

A. Yes. Algebra is very important.

B. But math is very difficult for me. I still have four years until graduation. Can I wait one more year and then take Algebra?

A. No, Alma. After Algebra, you'll be studying Geometry and Trigonometry. And you need those classes to take Physics.

B. I see. Then I think I should take Algebra next year. Thanks for explaining this, Ms. Franklin.

A. That's why I'm here, Alma.

TALK ABOUT IT

What do you think you'll be doing ten years from now? What kind of work will you be doing? What school subjects will you be using in your work? Share your future plans in pairs, in small groups, or as a class.

Do you sometimes meet with a guidance counselor? What do you talk about? Who helps you plan your course schedule?

ACT IT OUT!

With a partner, create a conversation between a guidance counselor and a student. They are planning the student's schedule for next year. Role-play your conversation for the class.

13

I'll Be Glad to Help

I	me	my	mine	myself
you	you	your	yours	yourself
he	him	his	his	himself
she	her	her	hers	herself
it	it	its	its	itself
we	us	our	ours	ourselves
you	you	your	yours	yourselves
they	them	their	theirs	themselves

A. What's **Johnny** doing?

B. **He's** getting dressed.

A. Does **he** need any help? I'll be glad to help **him**.

B. No, that's okay.   **He** can get dressed by **himself.**

1. *your husband fix the TV*

2. *your daughter feed the canary*

3. *your children cook breakfast*

4. *you and your husband clean the garage*

5. *your sister fix her car*

6. *your son take out the garbage*

7. *Bobby and Billy clean their bedroom*

8. *you do my homework*

9.

I Just Found This Watch

A. I just found this watch. Is it yours?

B. No, it isn't mine. But it might be **Fred's**. **He** lost **his** a few days ago.

A. Really? I'll call **him** right away.

B. When you talk to **him**, tell **him** I said "Hello."

1. *umbrella*
   Susan's

2. *briefcase*
   John's

3. *purse*
   Maria's

4. *wallet*
   George's

5. *camera*
   Mr. and Mrs. Green's

6. *notebook*
   Margaret's

7. *ring*
   Albert's

8. *cassette player*
   Bobby and Billy's

9. *address book*
   Edward's

10. *sneakers*
    Helen's

11. *glasses*
    Elizabeth's

12.

I Couldn't Fall Asleep Last Night

A. You look tired today.

B. Yes, I know.   I couldn't fall asleep last night.

A. Why not?

B. My **neighbors** were **arguing.**

A. How late did they **argue**?

B. Believe it or not, they **argued** until 3 A.M.!

A. That's terrible!   Did you call and complain?

B. No, I didn't.   I don't like to complain.

A. Well, I hope you sleep better tonight.

B. I'm sure I will.   My **neighbors** don't **argue** very often.

1. *neighbor's son practice the violin*

2. *neighbor's dog bark*

3. neighbor's daughter
   listen to her stereo

4. upstairs neighbors
   play cards

5. downstairs neighbors
   dance

6. neighbor across the hall
   sing

7. next door neighbors
   clean their apartment

8. neighbor's daughter
   play the piano

9. neighbor's son
   lift weights

10.

119

There's Something Wrong with My Washing Machine

something	anything
{ somebody } { someone }	{ anybody } { anyone }

A. There's something wrong with my **washing machine**.

B. I'm sorry. I can't help you. I don't know ANYTHING about **washing machines**.

A. Do you know anybody who can help me?

B. Not really. You should look in the phone book.* I'm sure you'll find somebody who can fix it.

*Or: You should look in the Yellow Pages.

1. *stove*

2. *TV*

3. *refrigerator*

4. *kitchen sink*

5. *bathtub*

6. *dishwasher*

7. *piano*

8. *radiator*

9.

Can You Send a Plumber?

A. Armstrong Plumbing Company. Can I help you?

B. Yes. There's something wrong with my kitchen sink. Can you send a plumber to fix it as soon as possible?

A. Where do you live?

B. 156 Grove Street in Centerville.

A. I can send a plumber tomorrow morning. Is that okay?

B. Not really. I'm afraid I won't be home tomorrow morning. I'll be taking my son to the dentist.

A. How about tomorrow afternoon?

B. Tomorrow afternoon? What time?

A. Between one and four.

B. That's fine. Somebody will be here then.

A. What's the name?

B. Helen Bradley.

A. And what's the address again?

B. 156 Grove Street in Centerville.

A. And the phone number?

B. 237–9180.

A. Okay. We'll have someone there tomorrow afternoon.

B. Thank you.

A. _____. Can I help you?

B. Yes. There's something wrong with my _____. Can you send a _____ to fix it as soon as possible?

A. Where do you live?

B. _____ in _____.

A. I can send a _____ tomorrow morning. Is that okay?

B. Not really. I'm afraid I won't be home tomorrow morning. I'll be _____ing.

A. How about tomorrow afternoon?

B. Tomorrow afternoon? What time?

A. Between _____ and _____.

B. That's fine. Somebody will be here then.

A. What's the name?

B. _____.

A. And what's the address again?

B. _____ in _____.

A. And the phone number?

B. _____.

A. Okay. We'll have someone there tomorrow afternoon.

B. Thank you.

1. _General Radio and TV Service_
   repair person

2. _Acme Electrical Repair_
   electrician

3. _Patty's Plumbing and Heating_
   plumber

TROUBLE WITH CARS

It might seem hard to believe, but my friends and I are all having trouble with our cars. There's something wrong with all of them!

Charlie is having trouble with his. The brakes don't work. He tried to fix them by himself, but he wasn't able to, since he doesn't know anything about cars. Finally, he took the car to his mechanic. The mechanic charged him a lot of money, and the brakes STILL don't work! Charlie is really annoyed. He's having a lot of trouble with his car, and he can't find anybody who can help him.

Betty is having trouble with hers. It doesn't start in the morning. She tried to fix it by herself, but she wasn't able to, since she doesn't know anything about cars. Finally, she took the car to her mechanic. The mechanic charged her a lot of money, and the car STILL doesn't start in the morning! Betty is really annoyed. She's having a lot of trouble with her car, and she can't find anybody who can help her.

Mark and Nancy are having trouble with theirs. The steering wheel doesn't turn. They tried to fix it by themselves, but they weren't able to, since they don't know anything about cars. Finally, they took the car to their mechanic. The mechanic charged them a lot of money, and the steering wheel STILL doesn't turn! Mark and Nancy are really annoyed. They're having a lot of trouble with their car, and they can't find anybody who can help them.

I'm having trouble with mine, too. The windows don't go up and down. I tried to fix them by myself, but I wasn't able to, since I don't know anything about cars. Finally, I took the car to my mechanic. The mechanic charged me a lot of money, and the windows STILL don't go up and down! I'm really annoyed. I'm having a lot of trouble with my car, and I can't find anybody who can help me.

✔ CHECK-UP

What's the Word?

1. Charlie tried to fix _____ car by _____.
2. Mark and Nancy's mechanic charged _____ a lot and still didn't fix _____ car.
3. Betty can't find anybody to help _____ fix _____ car.
4. I'm having trouble with _____ car, too. _____ starts in the morning, but the windows are broken.
5. The windows don't go up and down. I tried to fix _____ by _____, but I couldn't.
6. My friends and I can't fix _____ cars by _____ and we're all very angry at _____ mechanics.

Listening

I. Listen and choose the word you hear.

1. a. him   b. her
2. a. him   b. them
3. a. yours   b. hers
4. a. yourself   b. yourselves
5. a. them   b. him
6. a. our   b. her

II. Listen and choose what the people are talking about.

1. a. stove   b. sink
2. a. refrigerator b. stove
3. a. stereo   b. piano
4. a. camera   b. umbrella
5. a. dog   b. neighbor

How about YOU?

Are you "handy"? Do you like to fix things? Tell about something you fixed. What was the problem? How did you fix it? Also, tell about something you COULDN'T fix. What was the problem? What did you do?

For Writing and Discussion

THAT'S WHAT FRIENDS ARE FOR!

Frank has some very nice friends.   He sees his friends often.   When he needs help, they're always happy to help him.   For example, last week Frank moved to a new apartment.   He couldn't move everything by himself, and he didn't really have enough money to hire a moving company.   His friends came over and helped him move everything.   He was very grateful.   His friends said, "We're happy to help you, Frank.   That's what friends are for!"

Emma has some very special friends.   She sees her friends often.   When she needs help, they're always happy to help her.   For example, last month the faucet broke in Emma's kitchen and flooded her apartment.   There was water in every room.   She couldn't fix everything by herself, and her superintendent didn't help her at all.   Her friends came over and helped her fix the faucet and clean up every room in the apartment.   She was very grateful.   Her friends said, "We're happy to help you, Emma.   That's what friends are for!"

It's nice to have friends you can rely on when you need help.   Tell about a time when your friends helped you.   Tell about a time when you helped a friend.

SCHOOL CONNECTIONS: Offering and Asking for Help at School

A. What are you doing, Mr. Harper?

B. I'm putting the students' projects on the bulletin board.

A. Do you need any help?

B. That's okay, Omar. I can do it myself.

A. Are you sure, Mr. Harper? I'll be happy to help you.

B. All right, Omar. Thanks.

A. Do you know anything about the League of Nations?

B. Not really.

A. Do you know anybody who can help me? I have to do a report about the League of Nations for my social studies class.

B. You should go to the library. I'm sure the librarian can help you find some information.

A. Good idea. Thanks.

A. Excuse me. Do you have any books about the League of Nations?

B. I'm sure we do. Do you know how to use the on-line catalog?

A. No, I don't. Could you tell me how to use it?

B. Certainly. Push the *Reset* button. Then type *s*, the equals sign, and the subject you're looking for.

A. Thanks.

When do you offer help or ask for help at school? With a partner, role-play some situations for the class.

CHAPTER 1 *SUMMARY*

GRAMMAR

Like to

I We You They	like to	watch TV.
He She It	likes to	

I We You They	don't like to	watch TV.
He She It	doesn't like to	

Future: Going to

Am	I	
Is	he she it	going to eat?
Are	we you they	

Yes,	I	am.
	he she it	is.
	we you they	are.

No,	I'm	not.
	he she it	isn't.
	we you they	aren't.

Simple Past Tense

I He She It We You They	cooked spaghetti last night.

Indirect Object Pronouns

He's going to give	me him her it us you them	a present.

Time Expressions

I studied English	last week. last weekend. last month. last year.	last Sunday. last Monday. : last Saturday.	last spring. last summer. last fall (autumn). last winter.	last January. last February. : last December.

FUNCTIONS

Inquiring about Intention

Are you going to *cook spaghetti this week*?

What are you going to *give your wife for her birthday*?

Expressing Dislikes

I don't like to *cook spaghetti* very often.

Expressing Inability

I can't *give her a necklace.*

Suggesting

How about *flowers*?

Expressing Uncertainty

I don't know.

Attracting Attention

Harry!

Describing Feelings·Emotions

I'm really upset!

CHAPTER 2 *SUMMARY*

GRAMMAR

Count/Non-Count Nouns

There isn't any	bread. lettuce. flour.

There aren't any	apples. eggs. lemons.

How much	milk coffee ice cream	do you want?
How many	cookies french fries meatballs	

Not too	much.
	many.

Just	a little.
	a few.

FUNCTIONS

Suggesting

Let's *make sandwiches for lunch*!

Asking for and Reporting Information

There isn't any *bread*.
There aren't any *apples*.

My doctor says that *too many potatoes are bad for my health*.

Inquiring about Want-Desire

How much *milk* do you want?
How many *cookies* do you want?

Inquiring about Satisfaction

How do you like *the potatoes*?

Expressing Satisfaction

I think it's *delicious*.
I think they're *delicious*.

Offering

Would you care for some more?

Expressing Inability

We can't.

Expressing Gratitude

Thanks.

CHAPTER 3 *SUMMARY*

GRAMMAR

Count/Non-Count Nouns

Lettuce Butter Milk	is	very expensive this week.
Apples Carrots Onions	are	

Add	a little	salt. sugar. honey.
	a few	potatoes. nuts. raisins.

I recommend our	chocolate ice cream. scrambled eggs.

Everybody says	it's they're	delicious.

Partitives

a bag of flour	**a loaf of** bread
a bottle of soda	**a pound (lb.) of** butter
a box of cereal	
a bunch of bananas	**a bowl of** chicken soup
a can of beans	**a cup of** coffee
a half pound (half a pound) of cheese	**a dish of** ice cream
	a glass of milk
a head of lettuce	**an order of** scrambled eggs
a jar of jam	**a piece of** apple pie

Imperatives

Please **give me** a dish of ice cream.
Put a little butter into a saucepan.
Cook for 3 hours.

FUNCTIONS

Inquiring about Want-Desire

Do we need anything from *the supermarket*?

What would you like *for dessert*?

Expressing Want-Desire

We need *a loaf of bread*.

I'm looking for *a head of lettuce*.

Please give me *a dish of chocolate ice cream*.
I'd like *a glass of tomato juice*.

Asking for and Reporting Information

How much does *a head of lettuce* cost?
  Ninety-five cents.

Lettuce is very *expensive this week*.
Apples are very *expensive this week*.

There isn't any more *lettuce*.
There aren't any more *bananas*.

Everybody says *it's delicious*.

Expressing Surprise-Disbelief

NINETY-FIVE CENTS?!   *That's a lot of money!*

Asking for a Suggestion

What do you recommend?

Offering a Suggestion

I recommend *our chocolate ice cream*.

Inquiring about Satisfaction

How is *the vegetable soup*?

Expressing Satisfaction

It's *delicious*.

Instructing

Put a little butter into a saucepan.
Chop up a few onions.

Checking Understanding

A loaf of bread?
There isn't?
There aren't?

CHAPTER 4 SUMMARY

GRAMMAR

Future Tense: Will

(I will)	I'll	
(He will)	He'll	
(She will)	She'll	
(It will)	It'll	work.
(We will)	We'll	
(You will)	You'll	
(They will)	They'll	

I	
He	
She	
It	won't work.
We	
You	
They	

	I	
	he	
	she	
Will	it	arrive soon?
	we	
	you	
	they	

	I	
	he	
	she	
Yes,	it	will.
	we	
	you	
	they	

	I	
	he	
	she	
No,	it	won't.
	we	
	you	
	they	

Time Expressions

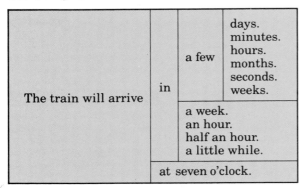

The train will arrive	in	a few	days. minutes. hours. months. seconds. weeks.
			a week. an hour. half an hour. a little while.
			at seven o'clock.

Might

I	
He	
She	
It	might clean it today.
We	
You	
They	

FUNCTIONS

Asking for and Reporting Information

Will *the train arrive* soon?
  Yes, *it* will.   *It'll arrive in five minutes.*

Inquiring about Probability

Do you think *it'll rain tomorrow*?

Expressing Probability

Maybe *it* will, and maybe *it* won't.

Expressing Possibility

I might *clean it today.*
You might *hurt your head.*

Inquiring about Intention

When are you going to *clean your apartment*?

Warning

Careful!
You might *hurt your head.*

Asking for Repetition

I'm sorry.   What did you say?

Expressing Gratitude

Thanks for *the warning.*

Extending an Invitation

Would you like to *go swimming* with me?

Accepting an Invitation

Okay.   I'll *go swimming* with you.

Declining an Invitation

No, I don't think so.

CHAPTER 5 *SUMMARY*

GRAMMAR

Comparatives

My new apartment is	colder larger bigger prettier	than my old apartment.
	more comfortable more attractive	

Should

Should	I he she it we you they	study?

I He She It We You They	should study.

Possessive Pronouns

This dog is much friendlier than	mine. his. hers. ours. yours. theirs.

FUNCTIONS

Describing

It was *fast/large/comfortable/interesting*.
My new _____ is *faster/larger/more comfortable/ more interesting*.

My dog isn't as *friendly* as *your dog*.
They aren't as *clean* as they used to be.

Bicycles are *safer* than *motorcycles*.
Yours is much *friendlier* than mine.

Asking for Advice

Should I *buy a bicycle or a motorcycle*?

Offering Advice

I think you should *buy a bicycle*.

Inquiring about an Opinion

Do you think *the weather in Miami is better than the weather in Honolulu*?

Expressing an Opinion

In my opinion, *New York is more interesting than San Francisco*.
I think *San Francisco is much more interesting than New York*.

Inquiring about Agreement

Don't you agree?

Expressing Agreement

That's right.
I agree.
I agree with you/him/her/John/. . . .
I think so.

Expressing Disagreement

I disagree.
I disagree with you/him/her/John/. . . .
No. I don't think so.

Asking for and Reporting Information

Why?
Why do you say that?
What makes you say that?
How come?

Initiating a Topic

You know, . . .

Inquiring about Certainty

Do you really think so?

Expressing Certainty

Definitely!

Expressing Dissatisfaction

I'm very upset about *the streets here in Brownsville*.

CHAPTER 6 *SUMMARY*

GRAMMAR

Superlatives

He's	the smartest the nicest the biggest the busiest	person I know.
	the most talented the most interesting	

FUNCTIONS

Describing

I think *your cousin* is very *kind/friendly/energetic/
generous.*
He's *the kindest/the friendliest/the most energetic/
the most generous* person I know.

This is the *smallest* one we have.

Expressing an Opinion

I think *your friend Margaret is very smart.*

Initiating a Topic

You know, . . .

Expressing Agreement

I agree.
You're right.

Offering to Help

May I help you?

Expressing Want-Desire

I want to buy *a small radio.*

Asking for and Reporting Information

Don't you have *a smaller one?*

Who is *the most popular actress in your country?*
What is *the best city in your country?*

Expressing Gratitude

Thank you anyway.

Apologizing

Sorry *we can't help you.*

CHAPTER 7 *SUMMARY*

GRAMMAR

Imperatives

Walk up Main Street.
Turn right.
Drive along Second Avenue to River Street.

FUNCTIONS

Asking for Directions

Can you tell me
Could you please tell me
Would you please tell me
   how to get to the laundromat from here?

Can you tell me how to get there?

What's the best/easiest/fastest/most direct/
   quickest/shortest way to get to *Peter's Pet Shop*?

Giving Directions

Walk up
Walk down } *Main Street.*
Walk along

You'll see the *laundromat* {on the right},
                 {on the left }

{
across from *the drug store.*
next to *the high school.*
between *the museum* and *the park.*
at the corner of *Brighton Boulevard*
   and *Twelfth Street.*
}

Walk up *Park Street* to *Second Avenue* and
{turn right.
{turn left.

Drive along *Second Avenue* to *River Street* and
{turn right.
{turn left.

Take *the Main Street bus* and get off at *First
   Avenue.*

Attracting Attention

Excuse me.

Expressing Gratitude

Thank you.
Thanks.
Thank you very much.
Thanks very much.
   You're welcome.

Asking for a Suggestion

Can you recommend *a good hotel*?

Describing

The Bellview is a good *hotel.*

I think it's one of the best *hotels* in *town.*

CHAPTER 8 *SUMMARY*

GRAMMAR

Adverbs

He works	slowly. terribly. sloppily. fast. hard. well.

Comparatives of Adverbs

He should try to work	more neatly. neater.
	more carefully. more politely.
	faster. harder. better.

Agent Nouns

dancer	skier
driver	teacher
painter	translator
player	worker
singer	

If-Clauses

If	I we you they	feel	better,	I'll we'll you'll they'll	go to work.
	he she it	feels		he'll she'll it'll	

If	I'm we're you're they're	tired,	I'll we'll you'll they'll	go to sleep early.
	he's she's it's		he'll she'll it'll	

FUNCTIONS

Describing

He's a *careless driver*.
He *drives* very *carelessly/slowly/fast/well/....*

Expressing an Opinion

I think *he's a careless driver*.

He should *try to speak slower*.

Expressing Agreement

I agree.
You're right.
You're probably right.

Asking for Feedback

Do I *type fast* enough?

Offering Feedback

You *type* too *slowly*.

Expressing Intention

I'll try to *type faster* in the future.
If *it rains*, I'll *take the bus*.

Inquiring about Intention

How are you going to *get to school tomorrow*?
What's *Fred* going to do *tomorrow*?
When are you going to *go to sleep tonight*?
What are you going to do *tonight* if *you have a lot of homework*?

Initiating a Topic

You know, . . .

Offering Advice

You shouldn't *drive so fast*.

Expressing Possibility

If you *drive too fast*, you might *have an accident*.

CHAPTER 9 *SUMMARY*

GRAMMAR

Past Continuous Tense

What	was	I he she it	doing?
	were	we you they	

I He She It	was	eating.
We You They	were	

Reflexive Pronouns

I You He She It We You They	took a walk by	myself. yourself. himself. herself. itself. ourselves. yourselves. themselves.

While-Clauses

I lost my wallet **while I was jogging through the park**.
He cut himself **while he was shaving**.

FUNCTIONS

Asking for and Reporting Information

What were you doing *last night at 8:00*?
What was *Doris* doing *last night* when *the lights
    went out*?

I saw *you yesterday*.
    When?
At about *2:30*.

Yesterday at 2:30 I was *cooking dinner*.

Which *apartment* do you live in?
    Apartment 1.

Were you *home at the time of the robbery*?
    No, I wasn't.   I was *washing my clothes at
        the laundromat*.

What did *the burglars take*?
    They took some money.
How much?
    About *three hundred dollars*.

What did you do yesterday?
Who did you *go bowling* with?

I had a bad day today.
    Why?   What happened?

I *lost my wallet* while I was *jogging through
    the park*.

Sympathizing

I'm sorry to hear that.
That's too bad.
How awful!
That's terrible!
What a shame!
What a pity!

Initiating a Topic

You look upset.

Admitting an Error

I guess I made a mistake.

CHAPTER 10 · *SUMMARY*

GRAMMAR

Could

Could	I he she it we you they	lift the suitcase?

Yes,	I he she it we you they	could.

No,	I he she it we you they	couldn't.

Be Able to

Was	I he she it	able to go swimming?
Were	we you they	

No,	I he she it	wasn't	able to.
	we you they	weren't	

Have Got to

I've We've You've They've He's She's It's	got to work.

I'll He'll She'll It'll We'll You'll They'll	be able to help you.

I He She It We You They	won't be able to help you.

Too + Adjective

He was too short. She was too busy.

FUNCTIONS

Inquiring about Ability

Could you *finish your homework last night?*
Were you able to *do the grammar exercises?*

Expressing Ability

I'm sure I'll be able to *move by myself.*

Expressing Inability

No, I couldn't.
No, I wasn't able to.

I couldn't do it.

He won't be able to *get to the airport on time.*
She can't *get into her apartment.*
He won't be able to *find a job.*
He couldn't *dance in the school play.*

Expressing Regret

I'm afraid *I won't be able to help you move
    tomorrow.*

Expressing Certainty

I'm sure *I'll be able to move by myself.*

Describing

I was too *short/sick/young/. . . .*

Inquiring about Satisfaction

Did you enjoy yourself *at the tennis match?*

Expressing Obligation

I had to *fix a flat tire.*

I've got to *take my son to the doctor.*

Describing Feelings-Emotions

George is upset/frustrated/disappointed.

CHAPTER 11 *SUMMARY*

GRAMMAR

Must

I He She It We You They	must work.

I He She It We You They	mustn't eat ice cream.

Count/Non-Count Nouns

Non-Count

He must eat	more less	bread. fish. meat.

Count

He must eat	more fewer	cookies. potatoes. eggs.

FUNCTIONS

Asking for Advice

Should I *stop eating rich desserts*?

What should I do?

Offering Advice

You should *go to my doctor.*

Inquiring about Obligation

Do you have to *stop eating ice cream*?

Expressing Obligation

You must *go on a diet.*
You must *stop eating rich desserts.*

I mustn't *eat as much ice cream as I did before.*

Asking for and Reporting Information

The doctor told *him he's a little too heavy.*

What did *the doctor* say?

Expressing Worry

I'm really worried about *your heart.*

Expressing Want-Desire

I want to *get a medical checkup.*

Greeting People

Hello, *Roger.*

CHAPTER 12 *SUMMARY*

GRAMMAR

Future Continuous Tense

(I will)	I'll	
(He will)	He'll	
(She will)	She'll	
(It will)	It'll	be working.
(We will)	We'll	
(You will)	You'll	
(They will)	They'll	

Time Expressions

I'll be staying	for	a few months. a few more hours. a few more minutes.
	until	Friday. 10 o'clock. I finish this.

We'll be arriving	at 7 A.M. in a few days.

FUNCTIONS

Asking for and Reporting Information

Will you *be home this evening*?
  Yes, I will.   I'll be *reading*.

I won't *be home this evening*.

How long will *your Aunt Gertrude be staying with
  us*?
How much longer will *you be working on my car*?
How late will *your husband be working tonight*?
Where will *you be getting off*?
When will *we be arriving in Paris*?
How far will *we be driving today*?
How soon will *Santa Claus be coming*?

Inquiring about Intention

How long will you *be staying with us*?

Expressing Intention

I won't *come over at five*.

Inquiring about Ability

When can you *come over*?

Expressing Ability

I can *come over at* _____ *o'clock*.

Offering a Suggestion

How about _____ *o'clock*?

Asking for Permission

Can I come over and visit this evening?

Inquiring about Agreement

Is that okay?
Will that be okay?

Expressing Agreement

Fine.
That'll be fine.

Greeting People

Hi, *Gloria*.   This is *Arthur*.

Hi, *Uncle Frank*!   How are you?
  Fine!

Leave Taking

Good-bye.
I'll see you then.
See you at *five*.

Offering to Help

I'll be glad to help.

Expressing Want-Desire

I want to *return the tennis racket I borrowed
  from you*.

Indicating Understanding

I see.

Initiating a Topic

By the way, . . .

CHAPTER 13 *SUMMARY*

GRAMMAR

Pronoun Review

Subject Pronouns	Object Pronouns	Possessive Adjectives	Possessive Pronouns	Reflexive Pronouns
I	me	my	mine	myself
you	you	your	yours	yourself
he	him	his	his	himself
she	her	her	hers	herself
it	it	its	its	itself
we	us	our	ours	ourselves
you	you	your	yours	yourselves
they	them	their	theirs	themselves

Some/Any

There's **something** wrong with my washing machine.
I'm sure you'll find **somebody/someone** who can fix it.

I don't know **anything** about washing machines.
Do you know **anybody/anyone** who can help me?

FUNCTIONS

Asking for and Reporting Information

There's something wrong with *my washing machine.*

Do you know *anybody who can help me?*

I won't *be home tomorrow morning.*
I'll be *taking my son to the dentist.*

Where do you live?
    156 Grove Street in *Centerville.*

What's the name?
    Helen Bradley.
And what's the address again?
    156 Grove Street in *Centerville.*
And the phone number?
    237–9180.

Offering to Help

Do you need any help?
Can I help you?
I'll be glad to help you.

Expressing Ability

I can *do my homework* by myself.

Expressing Inability

I can't *help you.*
I couldn't *fall asleep last night.*

Inquiring about Agreement

Is that okay?

Expressing Agreement

That's fine.

Expressing Disagreement

Not really.

Initiating a Topic

You look tired today.

Expressing Hope

I hope *you sleep better tonight.*

Expressing Regret

I'm afraid *I won't be home tomorrow morning.*

Offering Advice

You should *look in the phone book.*

Identifying

Armstrong Plumbing Company.

APPENDIX

Cardinal Numbers

1	one	20	twenty
2	two	21	twenty-one
3	three	22	twenty-two
4	four	.	.
5	five	.	.
6	six	29	twenty-nine
7	seven	30	thirty
8	eight	40	forty
9	nine	50	fifty
10	ten	60	sixty
11	eleven	70	seventy
12	twelve	80	eighty
13	thirteen	90	ninety
14	fourteen		
15	fifteen	100	one hundred
16	sixteen	200	two hundred
17	seventeen	300	three hundred
18	eighteen	.	.
19	nineteen	.	.
		900	nine hundred

1,000	one thousand
2,000	two thousand
3,000	three thousand
.	.
.	.
10,000	ten thousand
100,000	one hundred thousand
1,000,000	one million

Ordinal Numbers

1st	first	20th	twentieth
2nd	second	21st	twenty-first
3rd	third	22nd	twenty-second
4th	fourth	.	.
5th	fifth	.	.
6th	sixth	29th	twenty-ninth
7th	seventh	30th	thirtieth
8th	eighth	40th	fortieth
9th	ninth	50th	fiftieth
10th	tenth	60th	sixtieth
11th	eleventh	70th	seventieth
12th	twelfth	80th	eightieth
13th	thirteenth	90th	ninetieth
14th	fourteenth		
15th	fifteenth	100th	one hundredth
16th	sixteenth	1,000th	one thousandth
17th	seventeenth	1,000,000th	one millionth
18th	eighteenth		
19th	nineteenth		

How to read a date:
June 9, 1941 = "June ninth, nineteen forty-one"

Irregular Verbs: Past Tense

be	was	light	lit
begin	began	lose	lost
bite	bit	make	made
break	broke	meet	met
bring	brought	put	put
buy	bought	read	read
catch	caught	ride	rode
come	came	run	ran
cut	cut	say	said
do	did	see	saw
drink	drank	sell	sold
drive	drove	send	sent
eat	ate	shake	shook
fall	fell	sing	sang
feed	fed	sit	sat
feel	felt	sleep	slept
fight	fought	speak	spoke
find	found	stand	stood
fly	flew	steal	stole
forget	forgot	sweep	swept
get	got	swim	swam
give	gave	take	took
go	went	teach	taught
grow	grew	tell	told
have	had	think	thought
hear	heard	throw	threw
hurt	hurt	understand	understood
know	knew	wear	wore
lead	led	write	wrote
leave	left		

Tape Scripts for Listening Exercises

Chapter 1 – p. 7

Listen and choose the best answer.

1. What are you going to cook tomorrow?
2. What did you give your husband for his birthday?
3. When did you plant these flowers?
4. What do you do in the winter?
5. Where did your parents go on their vacation?
6. How often do they write to each other?
7. What did he send her?
8. When are you going to move?

Chapter 2 – p. 14

Listen and choose what the people are talking about.

1. A. How much do you want?
   B. Just a little, please.
2. A. Do you want some more?
   B. Okay. But just a few.
3. A. These are delicious!
   B. I'm glad you like them.
4. A. I ate too many.
   B. How many did you eat?
5. A. They're bad for my health.
   B. Really?
6. A. It's very good.
   B. Thank you.
7. A. Would you care for some more?
   B. Yes, but not too much.
8. A. There isn't any.
   B. There isn't?!

Chapter 3 – p. 20

Listen and choose what the people are talking about.

1. A. How much does a pound cost?
   B. A dollar forty.
2. A. How many loaves do we need?
   B. Three.
3. A. They're very expensive this week.
   B. You're right.
4. A. Sorry. There isn't any more.
   B. There isn't?
5. A. I need two quarts.
   B. Okay.

6. A. I bought too many.
   B. Really?
7. A. There weren't any in the refrigerator.
   B. Who ate them?
8. A. How much does the large box cost?
   B. Two nineteen.

Chapter 4 – p. 33

I. Mrs. Harris is calling Tommy and Julie's school. Listen and choose the correct lines for Mrs. Harris.

1. Hello. Park Elementary School.
2. Yes, Mrs. Harris. What can I do for you?
3. Oh? What's the matter?
4. That's too bad. Are you going to take them to the doctor?
5. Well, I hope Tommy and Julie feel better soon.

II. Choose the word you hear.

1. We'll be ready in half an hour.
2. I want to come to work today.
3. Don't smoke in here!
4. They'll work in their yard every Saturday.
5. Don't stand there! You might get hurt!
6. I call the doctor when I'm sick.
7. Careful! There are wet spots on the floor.
8. I'm sick and tired of sailing.

Chapter 5 – p. 41

Listen and choose what the people are talking about.

1. A. I think it should be shorter.
   B. But it's very short now!
2. A. I like it. It's fast.
   B. It is. It's much faster than my old one.
3. A. Why can't they be more polite?
   B. It isn't easy.
4. A. Is it reliable?
   B. Yes, but it isn't as reliable as my old one.
5. A. They aren't as good as they were last time.
   B. Don't worry. They'll be better next time.
6. A. Which one should I buy?
   B. Buy this one. It's more powerful than that one.

Chapter 6 – p. 52

Listen and choose the best answers to complete the commercial.

1. Good news for shoppers everywhere! Franklin's Department Store is having a big sale this week. Everything is on sale, and our products are very . . .
2. Our products are also better than items at other stores. Our clothes are more . . .
3. Our appliances are more . . .
4. And everybody agrees our salespeople are more . . .
5. Come on down to Franklin's Department Store! Don't shop at those other stores! We're the . . .

Chapter 7 – p. 62

I. Listen and choose the word you hear.

1. The school is on the right, next to the post office.
2. Walk up Town Road to Park Street.
3. Drive along Fourth Avenue to Station Street.
4. Take the subway to Bond Street.
5. The bus stop is at the corner of Main and Fifth.
6. Take this bus and get off at Rolling Road.

II. Where is the conversation taking place? Listen and choose.

1. A. Please give me an order of chicken.
   B. An order of chicken? Certainly.
2. A. Shh! Please be quiet! People are reading.
   B. Sorry.
3. A. Do you want to buy these clothes?
   B. Yes, please.
4. A. Can I visit my wife?
   B. Yes. She and the baby are in Room 407.
5. A. How much does one head cost?
   B. Seventy-nine cents.

Chapter 8 – p. 72

Listen and choose the best answer to complete the sentence.

1. If Ronald stays up late tonight . . .
2. If Barbara doesn't have enough money to pay the rent . . .
3. If the Watsons move to Arizona . . .
4. If I do my homework carelessly . . .
5. If Johnny doesn't feel better tomorrow . . .
6. If he doesn't translate accurately . . .

Chapter 9 – p. 83

Listen to the conversations. What happened to these people? Listen and choose the best answer.

1. A. How did you do that?
   B. I did it while I was shaving.
2. A. When did it happen?
   B. While I was getting off a bus.
3. A. What were they doing?
   B. They were playing outside.
4. A. Why do you think it happened?
   B. It was a very hot day.
5. A. The park isn't as safe as it used to be.
   B. I agree.

Chapter 10 – p. 89

Listen and choose the best answer.

1. I couldn't sit down.
2. We couldn't see the sun.
3. Did she enjoy the hamburger?
4. He wasn't able to lift it.
5. Why weren't the plumbers able to fix it?

Chapter 11 – p. 98

Listen and choose the best words to complete the sentences.

1. This tastes terrible. I used too much . . .
2. You know . . . the next time you bake this, you should try to use fewer . . .
3. You're a little too heavy. You must eat less . . .
4. This pie is delicious! I can't believe it has so many . . .
5. This tastes better than it did the last time I made it. I think it's because I used fewer . . .
6. Remember, we couldn't finish everything the last time we ate here. This time let's order less . . .

Chapter 12 – p. 113

Listen and choose the best answer.

1. When will we be arriving in Tokyo?
2. When will they be getting married?
3. How late did you work last night?
4. How much longer will the pies be baking?
5. Will they be leaving soon?
6. When will the boss be retiring?

Chapter 13 – p. 124

I. Listen and choose the word you hear.

1. Do you know him well?
2. Did you see them today?
3. Yours will be ready at five o'clock.
4. Careful! You might hurt yourselves!
5. I'll be glad to help him.
6. We're having trouble with her car.

II. Listen and choose what the people are talking about.

1. I'm going to have to call the plumber.
2. It's broken. It won't get cold.
3. She plays very well.
4. Careful! It's raining. Don't let it get wet!
5. He parked in the yard all night.

Glossary

The number after each word indicates the page where the word first appears.   Words introduced in Book 1 are not included in this list.
(adj) = adjective, (adv) = adverb, (n) = noun, (v) = verb

A

a while 92
able to 87
absolutely 32
accident 70
account 71
accurate 66
across the street 40
actually 110
add 22
address book 117
adult 113
advice 6
age 113
agree 43
ago 4
air conditioner 37
Alabama 6
all over 32
along 56
although 38
anniversary 6
annual 96
any more 28
anybody 120
anyone 120
anything 5
anyway 49
apart 6
appetite 20
apple 10
appliance 51
argue 118
Arizona 71
arm 32
around the corner
  40
ashamed 48
assistant 92
at all 83
attend 78
attractive 37
away 78
awful 98
awkward 68

B

back 102
bad luck 73
bag 14
baked (adj) 23
baking soda 22
ballet 91
bank account 71
bargain 51
be back 26
beans 10
because of 38
beef 98
beef stew 98
besides 51
best 49
better 41
black-and-white TV 39
blackout 76
block (n) 61
blood 83
blood pressure 100
blood test 100
bloody nose 103
bloom (v) 28
blueprints 98
boring 47
borrow 111
bottle 18
boulevard 63
bowl 21
box (n) 18
brakes (n) 123
break (v) 31
break into 78
brick 98
bright 47
broiled (adj) 23
build 98
bunch 18
burglar 78
burn (v) 80
bus system 38
butcher shop 56
butter 10

C

camera 117
can (n) 18
Canada 3
canary 116
candy store 58
capable 40
card player 66
cardiogram 100
care 15
career 113
careful 30
careless 66
carrot 18
carsick 31
cassette player 117
celery 10
cement 98
cents 19
change (v) 38
changes (n) 38
chapter 109
charge (v) 123
checkup 96
chess player 66
chest 100
chest X-ray 100
chicken 11
chicken soup 21
chocolate (adj) 13
chocolate cake 13
chocolate chip cookie 15
chop up 22
classmate 88
clumsy 93
coast 6
coffee pot 112
college student 78
color TV 39
come 29
come in 100
come over 107
complain 48
complete (adj) 100
completely 61

honest **39**
honey **22**
horseshoe **73**
hospitable **38**
hospital gown **100**
hot chocolate **21**
hour **22**
how far **109**
how late **109**
how long **109**
how much **12**
how much longer **109**
how soon **109**

I

ice **103**
if **69**
impolite **67**
in general **68**
indoors **28**
ingredients **98**
instead **32**
instructions **98**
intelligent **37**
intersection **83**
into **6**
itch (v) **73**
itself **79**

J

jail **26**
jam **10**
Japan **29**
jar **18**
jelly **10**
jog **77**
juice **10**
just **12**

K

key **93**
kind (adj) **48**
knife **73**
knit **112**

L

ladder **73**
lady **78**
last (v) **98**
last month **2**
last week **2**
last weekend **2**
last year **2**

Latin **39**
lazy **40**
lead (v) **100**
lean (adj) **96**
left **71**
leg **31**
lemon **11**
lend **6**
less **96**
lesson **89**
let's **11**
lettuce **11**
lift **87**
lift weights **119**
light (adj) **36**
light (n) **76**
like to **2**
lively **43**
loaf **18**
location **51**
lonely **71**
lose **6**
lose *his* job **6**
lose weight **99**
lost (adj) **61**
luck **73**
lungs **102**

M

machine **30**
magnificent **21**
main course **23**
margarine **97**
marry **27**
match (n) **88**
materials **98**
maybe **27**
mayonnaise **10**
mayor **38**
mean (adj) **48**
measles **32**
measure **100**
meat **14**
meatballs **12**
medical checkup **100**
melon **10**
merry-go-round **77**
Mexico **29**
middle-aged **113**
might **29**
might not **32**
mine **42**
Minnesota **6**
mirror **73**
miserable **48**
mix (in) **22**

mixing bowl **22**
modern **43**
moon **87**
more **37**
most **47**
motel **58**
motorcycle **39**
move away **100**
moving company **125**
museum **53**
mushroom **22**
must **96**
mustn't **99**
myself **79**

N

name (v) **29**
nauseous **32**
neat **41**
necktie **4**
need **18**
New Jersey **71**
news stand **58**
next door neighbor **119**
nightmare **70**
north **6**
nose **83**
notebook **117**
nurse **100**
nuts **22**

O

obnoxious **48**
ocean **87**
Ohio **78**
older **46**
omelette **11**
one **49**
onion **10**
open (v) **20**
operation **86**
opinion **43**
orange **11**
orange juice **10**
order (n) **21**
order (v) **23**
ours **42**
ourselves **79**
out of town **78**
outdoors **28**
over **73**
oversleep **71**
overtime **20**
overweight **97**
own (adj) **98**

P

package 80
pancakes 21
painter 66
painting (n) 6
patient (adj) 47
pepper 10
perfume 4
pet shop 58
Philadelphia 6
phone book 120
physical examination 97
piece 21
pipe 92
pizza 11
plant (n) 6
player 66
playground 57
plenty (of) 110
pneumonia 32
poke 82
police car 77
policeman 86
polite 38
positive 31
possible 121
potato 11
potato chips 96
pound (lb.) 18
pour (in) 22
powerful 37
pregnant 32
present (n) 4
price 52
probably 70
product 51
promise (v) 89
pronunciation 42
proud 48
pulse 100
puppy 29
put 22

Q

quart 18
quite 92

R

rainy 43
raisin 22
reach 109
ready 26
real 38
reasonable 52

receive 5
recipe 22
recommend 21
record player 50
relative 110
reliable 38
rent (n) 71
repair person 122
repair truck 92
require 98
retire 113
return 26
rice 10
rich 96
ridiculous 42
ring (n) 117
ripe 26
road 60
robbery 78
rocking chair 37
romantic 23
roommate 37
rub 103
rug 36

S

safe 36
safety glasses 30
salad 11
salespeople 51
salt 10
San Diego 6
San Francisco 43
sandwich 11
satisfied 41
saucepan 22
scale 100
scary 70
school play 93
scrambled eggs 21
seasick 31
season 28
second 26
sell 6
send 5
senior citizen 113
serious 102
several 110
shake *your* hand 100
shopping list 18
should 39
shoulder 73
shouldn't 70
side 92
sign (n) 83
silk (adj) 6

silver (adj) 6
since 123
sit down 20
skier 66
slice 22
sloppy 46
slow 66
smart 37
smoke (v) 30
snack foods 96
sneakers 117
snow (n) 28
snowy 43
soda 10
soft 36
some day 27
some more 13
somebody 73
someone 92
sometime 107
soup 18
south 6
spend 14
spicy 87
spill 73
spoon 73
sports car 36
spot 32
stadium 60
stay 109
stay up 71
steering wheel 123
step (v) 31
stethoscope 100
stew 22
stingy 47
stop (n) 61
stop (v) 83
stop sign 83
strawberry 21
stubborn 47
stupid 61
such 61
sugar 10
sunburn 31
superstition 73
superstitious 82
supposed to 98
Swiss cheese 19
sympathetic 41
symphony 88

T

table 23
take 78
take a ride 31

INDEX

12/
17
if
fine

2nd
Mow